DATE

GREEK PARTICLES IN THE NEW TESTAMENT
LINGUISTIC AND EXEGETICAL STUDIES

NEW TESTAMENT TOOLS
AND STUDIES

EDITED BY

BRUCE M. METZGER, Ph.D., D.D., L.H.D.

Professor of New Testament Language and Literature
Princeton Theological Seminary

VOLUME III

GRAND RAPIDS 3, MICHIGAN
Wm. B. EERDMANS
1962

GREEK PARTICLES IN THE NEW TESTAMENT

LINGUISTIC AND EXEGETICAL STUDIES

BY

MARGARET E. THRALL, Ph.D.

Assistant Lecturer in Hellenistic Greek
The University College of North Wales, Bangor

GRAND RAPIDS 3, MICHIGAN
Wm. B. EERDMANS
1962

TABLE OF CONTENTS

PREFACE

The term "particle" is capable of a fairly wide application. This study is in general confined to the paratactic conjunctions, to correlative particles such as μέν and τε, and to the adverbial particles expressing emphasis of one kind or another, such as γε and δή. The term may also be applied to the subordinating conjunctions and to the negatives οὐ and μή, but these have been omitted, as their investigation would have demanded the consideration of more extensive syntactical issues for which time and space were not available. [1] The particles treated here, therefore, are the ones which are dealt with in Denniston's study of classical usage. There are a few additions, however. Although the particle πλήν occurs as an independent conjunction in the classical period, it is not mentioned in Denniston. It is included here because its development in the κοινή is of linguistic interest and because its interpretation in two verses in Matthew is important exegetically. Also, some new connecting particles appear in the κοινή, formed from other parts of speech.

The New Testament particles are significant linguistically because they illustrate the usage of the κοινή, which differs in several ways from the classical idiom. The writers of the New Testament were not hampered in their manner of expression by the rigid adherence to classical models which characterizes many of the literary products of the Hellenistic period, and they are in some ways more useful than the papyri as a guide to the colloquial speech. Moreover there are various exegetical problems which may benefit from a more thorough investigation of the meaning of the particles in the verses concerned. Some scholars have claimed also that a wider exegetical interest attaches to some of the Marcan particles and that they are used throughout the Gospel in a rather artificial and arbitrary way to indicate psychological tension, allusion to the Old Testament, or the existence of a major turning-point in the narrative. These theories are on the whole more remarkable for their ingenuity than for their attention to linguistic

---

[1] Furthermore, a competent monograph dealing with several of these words has been published recently; it is A. C. Moorhouse's *Studies in the Greek Negatives*, Cardiff, 1959.

VII

detail, and they need to be carefully checked by means of strictly linguistic criteria.

The purpose of this monograph is twofold. The linguistic section supplies a more comprehensive classification and illustration of κοινή usage of particles than has been so far available, and attempts to assess the significance of the linguistic processes involved and to determine their causes. In the exegetical section I have tried to apply more exact linguistic criteria to various hypotheses involving particles and in some cases to suggest a new interpretation of difficult passages based on the exegesis of particles they contain.

I am indebted to my research supervisor, Professor C. F. D. Moule of Cambridge University, for a great deal of helpful criticism and advice.

M. E. T.

ABBREVIATIONS

Bauer-Arndt-Gingrich *A Greek-English Lexicon of the New Testament and Other Early Christian Literature*; A Translation and Adaptation of Walter Bauer's *Griechisch-Deutsches Wörterbuch zu den Schriften des Neuen Testaments und der übrigen urchristlichen Literatur* by William F. Arndt and F. Wilbur Gingrich, Cambridge and Chicago, [1957].

Denn. J. D. Denniston, *The Greek Particles*, 2nd edition, Oxford, 1954.

Mayser Edwin Mayser, *Grammatik der griechischen Papyri aus der Ptolemäerzeit*, II, 3, Berlin and Leipzig, 1934. (Where other volumes of this grammar have been used they are specifically mentioned).

PART ONE

THE LINGUISTIC SIGNIFICANCE OF GREEK PARTICLES IN THE NEW TESTAMENT

A. Introduction

The usage of particles in the New Testament may appear at first sight to have little significance from the linguistic point of view, since it shows hardly any developments which are not independently attested elsewhere. Uses peculiar to the New Testament, however, would not in fact possess much evidential value in any case. The greater their number, the less likely would it seem that they could be regarded as reflecting a genuine development of the Greek language in general, and the greater would be the probability that they should be attributed to the idiosyncrasies either of individual writers or of the early Christian community as a whole. The real significance of New Testament usage derives precisely from the fact that it is not unique but rather serves as a convenient focus for various tendencies seen elsewhere in the κοινή[1], and so provides a means of determining the nature of its divergence from the classical idiom.

This divergence consists of both degeneration and development. It is a process which has so far received inadequate treatment in the grammars available for the study of κοινή Greek, for while they provide information about the use or non-use of individual particles they are less satisfactory as a guide to the general linguistic developments which the individual uses illustrate. There is no complete classification of these tendencies, and some of the information offered is misleading. [2] Also, there is in some respects a deficiency

---

[1] I have adopted Robertson's definition of the term κοινή as including both the spoken and the written Greek of the Hellenistic period, excluding the literary Greek of the Atticistic revival (A. T. Robertson, *A Grammar of the Greek New Testament in the Light of Historical Research*, 5th edit., New York, 1931, p. 50).

[2] The only comment offered in Blass-Debrunner is that the New Testament is relatively deficient in particles by comparison with the classical idiom (Blass-Debrunner, *Grammatik des neutestamentlichen Griechisch*, 9th edit., Göttingen, 1954, §§ 107, 438). Mayser remarks on the decline of the classical collocations in the papyri, and implies that this is a general ten-

in the detailed evidence which is necessary in order to make possible a comparison either between κοινή and classical usage or between the different strata of the κοινή itself. Robertson [1] provides the fullest comment on the development of particles. He notes the decline of the adverbial particles, the fact that temporal adverbs tend to lose their temporal force and to become simply progressive, and the change in position of particles such as ἄρα and γε. But he does not specifically discuss the disappearance of the classical collocations, nor give any indication that some positive developments occurred which might be seen as counteracting, in some degree, the general impression of degeneration and decline, and his treatment of the tendencies apparent in the New Testament in relation to their contemporary context is somewhat cursory and haphazard. It may therefore prove useful to attempt a more comprehensive classification and discussion of the various ways in which the employment of particles in the κοινή differs from classical usage.

As the basis for such an investigation the New Testament writings possess certain advantages over the other contemporary documents available. They are more reliable than the papyri as an indication of the decline in the use of particles in the κοινή, for the deficiency in particles displayed by the papyri may be due in part to their subject matter or to their relative brevity rather than to the state of development of the language itself. Legal documents and official communications give little scope for variety of expression; the magical papyri consist mainly of invocations of demons, instructions and ingredients for charms, and various stereotyped formulas, and hardly give much indication of the

---

dency, but fails to consider whether any distinction should be made between the papyri and more literary productions (p. 169). Radermacher, as well as mentioning the general decline of the particles in the κοινή, maintains that dissatisfaction with certain simple forms of speech, now felt to be lacking in emphasis, led to their amplification by the addition of various connective or adverbial particles: thus, a simple καί became καί μέντοι or καί μήν καί, οὐδέ became οὐδὲ μήν, and the relative pronoun was often emphasized by περ (Ludwig Radermacher, *Neutestamentliche Grammatik*, Tübingen, 1925, pp. 37, 32-33). This assertion, however, needs some qualification and more discussion than Radermacher gives to it; many of the examples he quotes are classical collocations, and so can hardly be used as illustrations of a tendency peculiar to Hellenistic Greek. Also, if the tendency exists, it appears to contradict the opposite development noticed by Mayser, i.e. the decline in the use of combinations of particles in the papyri.

[1] *Op. cit.*, pp. 1144-1147.

way people would tell stories or conduct conversations; and the personal letters, which tend to be short, are inadequate for the purpose of displaying the whole range of their writers' vocabulary. The New Testament documents do not suffer from these disadvantages, as their subject matter is varied and gives more scope for whatever elegance of expression their authors are capable of, and most of them are considerably longer than the letters found among the papyri. They are also rather more useful than either the histories of Polybius or the recorded discourses of Epictetus, to take the two most typical representatives of the κοινή used by the literary classes. In the classical period, particles are more frequent and varied in conversational narrative than in formal history, [1] so that one might expect the author of Luke-Acts to prove a better guide than Polybius to the usage of the κοινή. The style of Epictetus is conversational, but has fewer new uses of particles than the New Testament; all the new uses found in Epictetus are found also in the New Testament, whereas the New Testament contains some additional ones which do not occur in the *Discourses*. [2]

B. CHARACTERISTICS OF NEW TESTAMENT USAGE

1. *Absence of Classical Combinations of Particles*

The comparative scarcity of particles in the New Testament is obvious. Mayser [3] points out that this is to a large extent due to the absence of the combinations of two or more particles which are characteristic of the classical idiom, more especially of the style of Plato, and which reappear in the works of the Atticists. [4] The difference, in this respect, between Plato and the writers of the New Testament is somewhat strikingly illustrated by a comparison between the New Testament as a whole and a single Platonic dialogue; the New Testament is rather more than ten times the length of the *Apology*, yet the *Apology* contains roughly twice as

---

[1] See Denn., p. lxxiv.

[2] ἄρα οὖν, ἀλλ' ἤ for ἀλλά, adverbial μενοῦν in the initial position, μέντοι γε, ἀλλά γε, καί γε.

[3] P. 169.

[4] It is this absence of several particles in combination which to a great extent accounts for the absence of adverbial particles noticed by Robertson, since particles such as γε, δή, and μήν are very frequently found in classical literature in combination with other particles.

many different combinations of particles. [1] As a further demonstration of the contrast between the New Testament and classical writers, and also as an indication of the way in which the Atticists revived the classical idiom, it is of interest to compare three works which provide us with a representative specimen of each of these literary groups and which also belong to approximately the same literary *genre*, i.e. historical narrative of the more informal and conversational type: Xenophon's *Institutio Cyri*, the Acts of the Apostles, and Philostratus's Life of Apollonius of Tyana. Acts is about the same length as the first book of the *Institutio Cyri*, yet Xenophon uses four times as many combinations of particles. It is almost twice as long as the first book of Philostratus's work, but Philostratus has more than three times as many classical combinations. [2] The following table shows the more exact figures upon which these comparisons are based:

	No. of pages in Teubner edit.	No. of combinations
Plato: *Apology*	47	40
New Testament	543	19
Xenophon: *Institutio Cyri* I	68	33
Acts	74	8
Philostratus: *Vita Apollonius* I	42	28

It is clear that in this respect the style of the New Testament writers differs radically from that of the classical authors and their Atticizing imitators. But it is a style which is typical of the products of the κοινή. In Mayser's section dealing with the use of particles in the papyri [3] he mentions or quotes only 29 combinations which are found in the papyri and also in classical literature. [4] As it is impossible to calculate the extent of the material which Mayser made use of, an exact comparison with classical writers is likewise impossible, but the papyri available to him, taken as a whole, would obviously be much more extensive in length than either of the single works of Plato and Xenophon already quoted, one of

---

[1] See Appendix, A, (i).

[2] See Appendix, A, (i).

[3] Pp. 114-174.

[4] See Appendix, A, (ii).

which contains 40 different combinations of particles, the other 33. It is possible, however, that this comparative deficiency in classical usage which is displayed by the papyri may be due in part to the nature of their subject matter. [1] In any case, there are other products of the κοινή which do not suffer from this disadvantage and which nevertheless exhibit a similar deficiency. The *Hermetica* and the *Discourses* of Epictetus both have fewer combinations of particles than the *Apology* or the first book of the *Institutio Cyri*, and yet they are considerably longer than either, as the accompanying table shows:

	No. of pages [2]	No. of combinations
Plato: *Apology*	47	40
Xenophon: *Institutio Cyri* I	68	33
Epictetus: *Discourses* I-IV	442	29 [3]
Hermetica	190	29 [3]

What was the reason for the decline in the use of combinations of particles? An obvious answer would be that it was the use of Greek as a common language by people of other linguistic traditions, whose own native languages were deficient in particles in general. This was doubtless an important contributory factor, but it does not seem to have been the only reason for the decay of the classical idiom. One would hardly expect it to have affected to any great extent the style of the Attic writers themselves. Yet Mayser remarks that the decline in particles begins with the New Comedy, [4] and a study of the use of combinations of particles by Menander, in contrast with the style of Aristophanes, substantiates this assertion. In the recently discovered *Dyskolos*, [5] 969 lines in length, there are 18 different combinations [6] and 41 occasions in all when particles are used in combination. But in the first 956 lines of the *Clouds* no fewer than 38 different combinations make their appearance, [7] and there are 69 occasions when a combination is used.

---

[1] See above, pp. 2-3.

[2] I have used the Budé edition of the *Hermetica*; the other figures are those for the Teubner editions of the works quoted.

[3] See Appendix, A, (ii).

[4] P. 169.

[5] Papyrus Bodmer IV, Ménandre, *Le Dyscolos* (Bibliotheca Bodmeriana, 1958).

[6] See Appendix, A, (iii).

[7] See Appendix, A, (iii).

The difference is appreciable, and must be attributed to some change in the Greek language in itself, quite apart from external linguistic influences.

This process of change is partly connected with the decline of the emphatic particles. [1] One might therefore suppose that it was simply the continuation of a process which had already begun. Denniston points out that in Homeric Greek "particles of emphasis . . . are heaped on in almost reckless profusion, and with but little definiteness of application." [2] In later Greek this lavish use of emphatic particles disappears. But it is important to notice the reason for its disappearance. The classical pruning of the Homeric particles was the result of a desire for greater exactness of expression. [3] This is hindered by a too lavish distribution of particles. But it can equally well be hindered by a deficiency of particles, since in that case there must be nuances and subtleties of thought which fail to receive adequate expression. One cannot therefore attribute the later decline of particles in the New Comedy and the κοινή to the same linguistic process which caused the change from the Homeric to the classical idiom. The two tendencies are in fact entirely opposed: one is an urge towards clarity, the other a disregard of the tools for expressing the finer shades of meaning. Is the second tendency simply one element in the passing of the classical age in general? Was the subtlety of thought achieved by the Athenian civilization at its height a unique phenomenon which was lost in the Hellenistic age? If the subtlety of thought itself disappeared, one might reasonably expect that the means of its expression would also die out.

Whatever the reason for it may be, the relative absence from the κοινή of the classical combinations of particles serves to distinguish it sharply from classical Greek. But there are also minor differences within the κοινή itself, and an examination of the numbers and the kinds of classical combinations which do make an appearance in the New Testament writings and the related literature may help to make clear which is the particular stratum of the κοινή to which the language of the New Testament belongs, and so to define its linguistic significance with rather more precision. For it is obvious that the κοινή was not at all uniform, and that its products

---

[1] See above, p. 1 n. 2.

[2] P. lxv.

[3] *Ibid.*

vary considerably in accordance with the degree of culture and education of their authors. [1] The New Testament provides us with examples of the contemporary language as it was used in conversation. (This is obvious in the case of the Epistles; but the Gospels and Acts, also, are narrative interspersed with conversation, and not formal history, so that one may count them as examples of the vernacular). But does it reflect the conversational usage of the educated classes or of the uneducated? At this point there seem to be differences of opinion. Moulton spoke of Luke as "a man of letters," [2] but de Zwaan disagreed with him. [3] As regards St. Paul, Robertson sets down almost side by side two completely contradictory opinions without appearing to notice the contradiction: he says first of all that Paul "thinks in Greek and it is the vernacular κοινή of a brilliant and well-educated man in touch with the Greek culture of his time," [4] and then proceeds to quote Deissmann, who sees Paul as "a non-literary man of the non-literary class in the Imperial Age," [5] The use by these writers of the classical combinations of particles may possibly provide a solution of the problem, since it offers an objective criterion of the extent of their education. The less educated a writer was, the fewer would be the combinations he would employ, since the general tendency was for them to disappear, and it was only an acquaintance with classical literature which caused their preservation and use.

As far as Pauline usage is concerned we have a profitable source of comparison in the *Discourses* of Epictetus, since there is a definite similarity between the style of Epictetus and the style of the major Pauline Epistles. The first book of the *Discourses* extends to 104 pages in the Teubner text, and the total number of pages for the Pauline corpus (excluding the Pastorals) is 110. Thus from the point of view of length, as well as of style, the conditions are convenient for making a comparison. When this is done we find that there is an appreciable difference between Epictetus and Paul in their use of the classical combinations: Epictetus has no

---

[1] See Ludwig Radermacher, *Koine*, Vienna, 1947, p. 17.

[2] Quoted by de Zwaan, see n. 3.

[3] J. de Zwaan, "The Use of the Greek Language in Acts," *The Beginnings of Christianity*, Pt. I (edit. F. J. Foakes Jackson and Kirsopp Lake), Vol. II, London, 1922, p. 40, n. 2.

[4] *Op. cit.*, p. 130.

[5] *Ibid.*, p. 131. See A. Deissmann, *Light from the Ancient East*, London, 1927, pp. 234-245.

fewer than 20, whereas Paul has only 12. [1] Now Epictetus was certainly acquainted with classical literature. Radermacher, however, is inclined to classify his language as a whole as belonging to the forms of speech of the less educated, since he professed to be a teacher of the lower classes as well as of those who had some claim to culture. [2] If this is a correct judgment, it may suggest that his use of particles in combination is somewhat more sparing than that of the literary classes in general, since he would be more concerned to accommodate his language to the vulgar speech in which such combinations were infrequent. But if the idiom of Epictetus is in this respect in some measure inferior to that of the best educated classes of society, it is clear that the Pauline idiom is very much more so. This conclusion would appear to favor Deissmann's opinion of Paul, as being typical of the non-literary class.

Luke's Greek is a little more difficult to assess according to this criterion, since it is less easy to find a suitable basis of comparison. The histories of Polybius are altogether more formal in style than the Lucan writings. However, since Luke claims, at least, to write as an historian, [3] these are perhaps as suitable for the purpose as any other specimen of the literary κοινή. The first book of Polybius occupies 120 pages in the Teubner edition, and contains 13 classical combinations of particles. [4] The book of Acts [5] is 74 pages long, and has 8 different combinations. [6] In proportion to its length, therefore, it has the same number of combinations as Polybius I, i.e. one new combination to every 9 pages, and this would suggest that the author's level of culture and education was much the same as that of Polybius. There are, however, several other factors to be taken into consideration. Acts is a more informal and conversational type of narrative, so that one would expect a higher proportion of particles than in Polybius. Moreover, two of the classical combinations in Acts occur only once each (ἄρα γε, xvii 27; ἄρά γε, viii 30), and those that remain are very common ones. Finally,

---

[1] See Appendix, A, (iv).

[2] *Koine*, p. 65.

[3] See the commentary on the Lucan preface by H. J. Cadbury in Foakes Jackson and Lake, *Beginnings*, Pt. I, Vol. II, pp. 489-510.

[4] See Appendix, A, (iv).

[5] The Gospel is less suitable for investigation in this connection, since Luke is copying at any rate one earlier written source and possibly two, and not writing freely in his own style to the same extent as he does in Acts.

[6] See Appendix, A, (i).

Polybius is fond of combinations of particles which include μήν. These are a characteristic of classical literature but tend to disappear in the κοινή, [1] and Luke does not use them at all. These considerations perhaps indicate that Luke's Greek is of a less literary quality than that of Polybius, and so suggest that the author of Acts was of a somewhat lower level of education.

Since Luke and Paul are two of the most fluent and idiomatic of the New Testament writers, it is plain that the language of the New Testament as a whole does not reflect the κοινή as it was used by the best educated classes in Hellenistic society, those classes, that is to say, who were well acquainted with the idioms of classical literature. The one possible exception is the Epistle to the Hebrews. In a total of 20 pages there are no fewer than 9 combinations of particles which occur in classical literature. [2] This is a large number in comparison with the length of the book, and suggests that Hebrews may be more typical of the cultured speech of the educated classes than any of the other documents in the New Testament. For the most part, when one has discounted certain idioms either derived from the Septuagint or due to the influence of Aramaic, the New Testament shows us the κοινή in the process of free and natural development, unrestrained by conformity to classical habits of speech.

2. New Combinations of Particles

A few post-classical combinations of particles make their appearance in the New Testament. They do not occur in sufficient numbers to offset the decline in the use of the classical combinations, but as some of them are found elsewhere in the κοινή the tendency may be worth mentioning.

a. εἰ δὲ μή γε

This phrase is found five times in Luke, and would seem to be a characteristic of the Gospel's style. As an example we may quote Lk. x 6: καὶ ἐὰν ἐκεῖ ᾖ υἱὸς εἰρήνης, ἐπαναπαήσεται ἐπ' αὐτὸν ἡ εἰρήνη ὑμῶν· εἰ δὲ μή γε, ἐφ' ὑμᾶς ἀνακάμψει. The other examples occur in the following passages: v 36; v 37; xiii 9; xiv 31-32. There are three other instances in the New Testament: Mt. vi 1; ix 17; II Cor. xi 16.

---

[1] γε μήν does not occur in the papyri, the *Hermetica*, or Epictetus; καὶ μήν is absent from the *Hermetica* and the papyri.

[2] See Appendix, A, (iv).

The phrase εἰ δὲ μή, meaning "but if not," "otherwise," is a classical idiom, e.g. μάλιστα μὲν ὡς καὶ ξύμφορα δέονται, εἰ δὲ μή, ὅτι γε οὐκ ἐπιζήμια (Thuc. I 32; cf. I 28, 131; Pl. *Phd.* 91 C). In classical Greek, however, it is left unemphasized. In the κοινή it is found emphasized by γε in Epictetus, Polybius, and the papyri, e.g. ἐν ἀρχῇ οὐκ ἔστιν. εἰ δὲ μή γε, ἔδει τοὺς δὶς καὶ τρὶς ὑπάτους εὐδαίμονας εἶναι· οὐκ εἰσὶ δέ (Epict. *Dss.* III 22, 27); σχεδὸν γὰρ πάντων, εἰ δὲ μή γε, τῶν πλείστων συγγραφέων... (Polyb. III 58); περὶ δὲ τῆς θεραπείας πειρασόμεθα μὲν χαλκιαίους, εἰ δὲ μή γε, διχαλκιαίους (Zen. P. 59019, 5).[1] It occurs twice in the Septuagint (Dan. iii 15; Bel 8), once in II Clement (vi 7) and once in the Didache (xi 9). One cannot be sure, however, that the use of particles in the Apostolic Fathers is independent of their use in the New Testament, so that these last two instances are not necessarily separate witnesses to the use of εἰ δὲ μή γε in the κοινή.

There are two possible reasons for the addition of γε to the classical εἰ δὲ μή. It may have been the result of a desire for greater emphasis; Radermacher maintains that at this period simple negatives were thought to sound weak.[2] There was also a tendency to avoid hiatus,[3] which might have been operative in the examples quoted from Luke and Epictetus.

b. ἄρα οὖν

In the New Testament this combination is peculiar to the Pauline Epistles. It occurs frequently in Romans, e.g. τῷ Μωϋσεῖ γὰρ λέγει· ἐλεήσω ὃν ἂν ἐλεῶ, καὶ οἰκτιρήσω ὃν ἂν οἰκτίρω. ἄρα οὖν οὐ τοῦ θέλοντος οὐδὲ τοῦ τρέχοντος, ἀλλὰ τοῦ ἐλεῶντος θεοῦ (Rom. ix 15-16). The other examples occur as follows: Rom. v 18; vii 3, 25; viii 12; ix 18; xiv 19; Gal. vi 10; I Thess. v 6; II Thess. ii 15. There may be two further instances, but in each case the text is uncertain: in Rom. xiv 12 οὖν is omitted by B D* G 1739, and in Eph. ii 19 οὖν is omitted in P46 G Ψ 1739 Or. In view of the infrequency of ἄρα οὖν elsewhere, it is probably the correct reading in both instances.

The purpose of the combination is presumably to provide an emphatically inferential connective. In itself the particle ἄρα may possess either an adverbial force, expressing interest or surprise,[4]

---

[1] Mayser, p. 124.
[2] *Gramm.*, p. 32.
[3] *Ibid.*, pp. 35-36.
[4] See Denn., pp. 33-40; in the N.T., Lk. xxii 23; Acts xii 18.

or a connective sense, implying consequence. [1] However, where Paul uses it at the beginning of a sentence it is always connective. [2] It seems probable, therefore, that both particles in the combination are intended to imply logical connection, the one simply reinforcing the other. It is several times used by Paul to sum up the argument of a whole section (rather than merely indicating the logical consequence of the immediately preceding sentence considered in isolation), Rom. v 18; vii 25; viii 12; xiv 19; Gal. vi 10.

Outside the New Testament it is rare, but there are one or two occurrences. In one of the Hermetic writings it is used in the same way as in the Pauline Epistles, to sum up the thought of the preceding section as a whole: ὅσαις ἂν οὖν ψυχαῖς ὁ νοῦς ἐπιστατήσῃ, ταύταις φαίνει ἑαυτοῦ τὸ φέγγος, ἀντιπράσσων αὐτῶν τοῖς προλήμμασιν. ὥσπερ ἰατρὸς ἀγαθὸς λυπεῖ τὸ σῶμα προειλημμένον ὑπὸ νόσου, καίων ἢ τέμνων, τὸν αὐτὸν τρόπον καὶ ὁ νοῦς ψυχὴν λυπεῖ, ἐξυφαιρῶν αὐτὴν τῆς ἡδονῆς, ἀφ' ἧς πᾶσα νόσος ψυχῆς γίνεται· νόσος δὲ μεγάλη ψυχῆς ἀθεότης, ἔπειτα δόξα, αἷς πάντα τὰ κακὰ ἐπακολουθεῖ καὶ ἀγαθὸν οὐδέν· ἆρ' οὖν ὁ νοῦς ἀντιπράσσων αὐτῇ τὸ ἀγαθὸν περιποιεῖται τῇ ψυχῇ, ὥσπερ καὶ ὁ ἰατρὸς τῷ σώματι τὴν ὑγίειαν (Herm. I xii 3). There are also two or three examples in the Apostolic Fathers: II Clem. xiv 3, 4 (the second example occurs at the beginning of an apodosis); Barn. x 2 (here the force of the combination seems to be inceptive rather than inferential); Ign. ad Trall. xi.

c. ἀλλά γε καί, ἀλλά μενοῦν γε καί

The first of these combinations occurs in Lk. xxiv 21, the second in Phil. iii 8. Neither appears to be attested elsewhere, so that one might argue that they are nothing more than momentary idiosyncrasies on the part of Luke and of Paul respectively, and thus of no significance for the study of the κοινή in general. On the other hand, if the use of particles in the New Testament for the most part reflects that of the κοινή, it is just possible that a particle or combination of particles which is peculiar to the New Testament may in fact represent an idiom which was current at the time but which does not happen to have emerged to view in any of the other contemporary documents. This is a feasible hypothesis only if the idiom in question is used by more than one writer, and if the

---

[1] See Denn., pp. 40-41.
[2] Rom. x 17; I Cor. xv 18; II Cor. v 14; vii 12; Gal. vi 10.

possibility of derivation from the Septuagint is excluded. In the case of ἀλλά γε καί and ἀλλά μενοῦν γε καί the second of these conditions is obviously fulfilled, since neither phrase occurs in the Septuagint at all. The first condition would also appear to be fulfilled, since it is probable that the two combinations are essentially the same, i.e. a basic ἀλλά καί reinforced by an emphatic particle or particles, and that we have a single idiom attested both by Luke and by Paul. This last assertion, however, needs further substantiation.

In Luke, ἀλλά γε καί is found in the story of the Resurrection appearance to the two disciples on the road to Emmaus. After they have spoken of the crucifixion of Jesus and the consequent destruction of their own hope that he was the Messiah, they continue, ἀλλά γε καὶ σὺν πᾶσιν τούτοις τρίτην ταύτην ἡμέραν ἄγει ἀφ' οὗ ταῦτα ἐγένετο. As a combination of three particles, each one integrally connected with the other, ἀλλά γε καί is nowhere attested. On the other hand, to give a separate value to each of the particles individually hardly serves to clarify the sense, and it is not Luke's habit to scatter particles about in an indefinite fashion with no precise application. It seems likely, therefore, that what we have here is a basic combination of two particles, with a meaning already established, to which Luke has added a third. Theoretically there are three possibilities:

(i)   a basic combination γε καί, preceded by ἀλλά,
(ii)   ἀλλά γε as the primary combination, reinforced by καί,
(iii) ἀλλά καί as the basic group, with the insertion of γε for the sake of extra emphasis.

The first of these has the least to be said for it. There is no warrant, either in classical Greek or in the κοινή, for the use of γε καί as a combination of particles with an independent significance. When the two words do occur in juxtaposition the collocation is fortuitous and the particles function separately: γε modifies the preceding word and καί the word following, e.g. ὅσον γε καὶ ἡμᾶς εἰδέναι (Polyb. I 4, 3; see also IV Macc. vi 34; xiv 11, 14, 19). [1]

---

[1] There is a slightly different use of γε καί in Philostratus, *Vit. Ap.* viii 12 (οὐ γὰρ ἀνήσει ἐρωτῶν τὰ σά, ὅς γε καὶ πρὸ πεντεκαίδεκα ἴσως ἡμερῶν ἐμοὶ ξυμπίνων . . .), where καί can hardly be regarded as modifying the following phrase, so that it might be thought to cohere with the preceding γε. But the more probable explanation is that both particles separately modify the relative pronoun, γε with a limiting force and καί indicating that

The second possibility is somewhat more likely than the first. The combination ἀλλά γε is infrequent, but there are one or two instances of its occurrence. Denniston [1] quotes a fragment of Gorgias, ἀλλά γε τὸ φῶς πολεμεῖ τοῖς τοιούτοις (Gorg. *Fr.* 11a. 10). There is also an example in the New Testament itself, εἰ ἄλλοις οὐκ εἰμὶ ἀπόστολος ἀλλά γε ὑμῖν εἰμι (I Cor. ix 2). [2] Moreover, the use of the combination ἀλλά . . . γε is frequent in the classics, [3] and there was a general tendency in the κοινή to change combinations such as καὶ . . . γε, καίτοι . . . γε, μέντοι . . . γε so that the two particles were immediately juxtaposed, [4] and the same thing may have happened occasionally with ἀλλά . . . γε. In the specific passage under consideration, however, there are two difficulties in the way of supposing ἀλλά γε to be the basic group of particles. The classical combination ἀλλά . . . γε is always adversative, and presumably ἀλλά γε would have a similar force (as it does in the Gorgias fragment, the Pauline instance, and the example in Polybius), whereas in Lk. xxiv 21 the following σὺν πᾶσιν τούτοις would appear to demand a progressive sense for the introductory particles. Secondly, the addition of καί to ἀλλά γε seems unlikely, supposing ἀλλά γε to be adversative. It might perhaps adhere not to ἀλλά γε but to σὺν πᾶσιν τούτοις, but this phrase hardly seems to need any additional emphasis.

The third form of division is to take ἀλλά καί as the basic combination. This is preferable for two reasons. First, ἀλλά καί occurs more frequently than ἀλλά γε. Although it is not a common idiom in classical literature, it is found occasionally, in a progressive sense, [5] in Xenophon, Demosthenes, and Hippocrates, e.g. καὶ εἰμὶ νῦν μὲν τυράννῳ ἐοικώς, τότε δὲ σαφῶς δοῦλος ἦν· καὶ τότε μὲν ἐγὼ φόρον ἀπέφερον τῷ δήμῳ, νῦν δὲ ἡ πόλις τέλος φέρουσα τρέφει με. ἀλλά καί Σωκράτει, ὅτε μὲν πλούσιος ἦν, ἐλοιδόρουν με ὅτι συνῆν, νῦν δ᾽ ἐπεὶ πένης

---

the content of the relative clause forms a significant addition to the content of the main sentence.

[1] P. 23.

[2] See also Polyb. XII 4, 10 οὐ δύνανται ταῦτα κατὰ γένη τηρεῖν, ἀλλά γε συμπίπτει . . . ἀλλήλοις and cf. Arrian, *de Cyneg.* xv 1, although here the reading is uncertain.

[3] See Denn., p. 12.

[4] See below, pp. 37-38.

[5] Progressive ἀλλά καί, formed by the addition of an emphasizing καί to progressive ἀλλά, is to be distinguished from ἀλλά καί preceded by an οὐ μόνον clause, which is very much more frequent.

γεγένημαι, οὐκέτι οὐδὲν μέλει οὐδενί (Xen. *Conv*. iv 32). [1] As a witness to the use of progressive ἀλλὰ καί in the κοινή there is the following example from the papyri: τῶν δού[λω]ν τοὺς χρηματισμοὺς ἕως τούτου οὐχ εὗρον, . . . καὶ ὁ Ἀχιλλ[εὺ]ς δὲ ἀποδημεῖ, καὶ ἐπὶ τῶι πράγματι ἀμηχανῶ . . . ἀλλὰ [κ]αὶ ὁ ἀγορά[σας] παρὰ σοῦ τὸ ἄλλο σωμάτιον, . . . ἠγνωμόνησεν (P. Giess. 20). [2] It is found also in the *Discourses* of Epictetus: I 1, 20; 27, 5; IV 1, 8. Finally, there are no fewer than five occurrences in the Epistle of Barnabas: vii 3; ix 4, 6; x 6, 8. In the Third Gospel itself there are at least two examples in addition to the verse under consideration. The first is found in Lk. xvi 20-21: πτωχὸς δέ τις ὀνόματι Λάζαρος ἐβέβλητο πρὸς τὸν πυλῶνα αὐτοῦ εἱλκω-μένος καὶ ἐπιθυμῶν χορτασθῆναι ἀπὸ τῶν πιπτόντων ἀπὸ τῆς τραπέζης τοῦ πλουσίου· ἀλλὰ καὶ οἱ κύνες ἐρχόμενοι ἐπέλειχον τὰ ἕλκη αὐτοῦ. The particle ἀλλά must here be regarded as progressive, since the sentence it introduces has no adversative connection with the preceding one, but simply expresses an additional element in the poor man's distress. The following καί must cohere with ἀλλά and reinforce it. To regard καί as attached to οἱ κύνες with the meaning of "also" or "even" would make no sense, as no other agents of the poor man's misery have been specifically mentioned, and it is not likely simply to emphasize οἱ κύνες, since the other instances of purely emphatic καί in Luke all precede personal or demonstrative pronouns (Lk. iii 14; xix 42; xxii 56, 59). The two particles are therefore combined in a progressive sense, "further," "what is more." The second Lucan example of the idiom occurs in the Emmaus story (xxiv 22): after the two disciples have remarked that it is now three days since Jesus was crucified (with the implication, presumably, that nothing has happened, despite his previous predictions of resurrection), they continue: ἀλλὰ καὶ γυναῖκές τινες ἐξ ἡμῶν ἐξέστησαν ἡμᾶς, γενόμεναι ὀρθριναὶ ἐπὶ τὸ μνημεῖον· καὶ μὴ εὑροῦσαι τὸ σῶμα αὐτοῦ ἦλθον λέγουσαι καὶ ὀπτασίαν ἀγγέλων ἑωρακέ-ναι, οἳ λέγουσιν αὐτὸν ζῆν. καὶ ἀπῆλθόν τινες τῶν σὺν ἡμῖν ἐπὶ τὸ μνημεῖον, καὶ εὗρον οὕτως καθὼς καὶ αἱ γυναῖκες εἶπον, αὐτὸν δὲ οὐκ εἶδον. Again, it makes no sense to attach καί to the following word. There is no reason to emphasize the fact that the first visitors to

---

[1] See also Xen. *Instit. Cyri* VIII viii 17-19; Dem. xix 54, 257, 258; Hipp. *Mul.* 188, *Vict.* 93, *Gland.* 16.

[2] A. S. Hunt and C. C. Edgar, *Select Papyri* (Loeb ed.), London and New York, 1932, No. 117.

the empty tomb were women, nor is there any warrant for translating "even certain women," or "certain women also," as though some other persons had previously been mentioned as doing the same thing. If, however, the καί adheres to the preceding ἀλλά, the ἀλλά must be understood in a progressive sense, reinforced by καί, since an adversative ἀλλά followed by καί and meaning "but also" is possible only when preceded by an οὐ μόνον clause. (Plummer [1] treats the verse as expressing a "favourable item" of information, and so feels bound to regard ἀλλά as adversative. But the conclusion of the story is not the words οἱ λέγουσιν αὐτὸν ζῆν but αὐτὸν δὲ οὐκ εἶδον in the following verse, and it is more likely that these are the words which carry the emphasis, and that the whole section is a further example of the disciples' fundamental lack of faith. It is at this point that Jesus begins to reproach them for their stupidity and their slowness to believe the prophets).

In view of these two examples of progressive ἀλλά καί in Luke, and of the fact that there are several other instances of its use both in classical Greek and in the κοινή, it is more probable as the basic combination in Lk. xxiv 21 than ἀλλά γε, which occurs nowhere else in Luke—Acts and is in general less frequent. The second argument in its favor is simply that it provides the progressive introduction, "moreover," which appears to be demanded by σὺν πᾶσιν τούτοις. If this interpretation is correct, the γε which separates the two particles that form the basic group will serve to give added emphasis. The reason for its insertion between ἀλλά and καί may possibly be that Luke uses the combination καί γε elsewhere [2] and so would have thought it misleading here to add the γε after the καί.

The Pauline example of ἀλλά καί further reinforced is found in Phil. iii 7-8: ἀλλὰ ἅτινα ἦν μοι κέρδη, ταῦτα ἥγημαι διὰ τὸν Χριστὸν ζημίαν, ἀλλὰ μενοῦν γε καὶ ἡγοῦμαι πάντα ζημίαν εἶναι διὰ τὸ ὑπερέχον τῆς γνώσεως Χριστοῦ Ἰησοῦ τοῦ κυρίου μου. The καί before ἡγοῦμαι is omitted by P⁴⁶ ℵ* 1739 f vg Copˢᵃ, but this is obviously an attempt to simplify what appears at first sight to be an extremely cumbersome group of particles. That the original combination was progressive ἀλλά καί seems to be probable in the light of an earlier instance in the first chapter of the Epistle: καὶ ἐν τούτῳ χαίρω·

---

[1] Alfred Plummer, *A Critical and Exegetical Commentary on the Gospel according to St Luke*, Edinburgh, 1896, *in loc.*

[2] See Acts ii 18; xiv 17; xvii 27.

ἀλλὰ καὶ χαρήσομαι (Phil. i 18). Here ἀλλὰ καί is clearly progressive, and this is a verse which resembles iii 8 in construction, since in both we have the repetition in the second clause of a word or words from the first, with the same verb used in a different tense. If this comparison is valid, we have in Phil. iii 8 a basic ἀλλὰ καί, in a progressive sense, reinforced by a combination of emphatic particles, μενοῦν γε.

Thus, it is at least possible that there was a tendency in the κοινή in general to make progressive ἀλλὰ καί still more emphatic by the addition of another particle or even of several other particles.

3. Extensions of Meaning

While some of the classical particles disappear altogether in the κοινή, there are others which extend their original function. The New Testament supplies two examples of this process.

a. ἀλλ' ἤ for ἀλλά

This idiom is found only once, in Lk. xii 51: δοκεῖτε ὅτι εἰρήνην παρεγενόμην δοῦναι ἐν τῇ γῇ; οὐχί, λέγω ὑμῖν, ἀλλ' ἤ διαμερισμόν. The classical use of ἀλλ' ἤ is inadequate to explain its significance here. According to Denniston, [1] this classical idiom may be divided into the following three categories.

(i) A negation which contains a word of comparison (some part of ἄλλος) is followed by an exception, e.g. ὥστε μηδὲν ἄλλο δοκεῖν εἶναι ἀληθὲς ἀλλ' ἤ τὸ σωματοειδές (Pl. Phd. 81 B). This is of no assistance in elucidating Lk. xii 51, since ἀλλ' ἤ is not there preceded by any word of comparison.

(ii) A negation which does not contain a word of comparison may be followed by an exception introduced by ἀλλ' ἤ, e.g. μηδετέρους δέχεσθαι ἀλλ' ἤ μιᾷ νηὶ ἡσυχάζοντας (Thuc. III 71). Again, this hardly explains the Lucan instance. The fact that the coming of Christ will produce dissension is in no way an exception to the previous assertion that he has not come to bestow peace.

(iii) Instead of a general negation, which has to be supplied in thought, a particular instance of it is given, e.g. ἔστι δ' ὁ μὲν ἱέραξ γαμψώνυχος, ὁ δὲ κόκκυξ οὐ γαμψώνυχος· ἔτι δὲ οὐδὲ τὰ περὶ τὴν κεφαλὴν ἔοικεν ἱέρακι . . . ἀλλ' ἤ κατὰ τὸ χρῶμα μόνον προσέοικεν ἱέρακι (Aristot. de Anim. Hist. 563 b 19). The second half of this Denniston would

---

[1] Pp. 24-26.

translate: "Nor is the cuckoo like the falcon in the head either: (indeed there is no likeness) except that it is like the falcon in colour only." [1] It would be theoretically possible to fit the Lucan ἀλλ' ἤ into this category, supplying the general negation, "I have not come for any purpose at all," so that we could then paraphrase the second half of the verse: "I have not come to bring peace: (indeed I have come for no purpose at all) except to bring dissension." But it seems very unlikely that Luke intended to represent Christ as saying that the sole purpose of his mission was to produce dissension.

The obvious explanation is that Luke is using ἀλλ' ἤ simply as the equivalent of ἀλλά. On the other two occasions of the use of the phrase οὐχί, λέγω ὑμῖν (Lk. xiii 3-5; cf. xvi 30) ἀλλά introduces the following clause, and the fact that some witnesses (P⁴⁵ D Θ) read ἀλλά instead of ἀλλ' ἤ in Lk. xii 51 shows that the logical relation between the two clauses was felt to be that which was normally expressed by using ἀλλά as a connective.

The Lucan use of ἀλλ' ἤ illustrates a tendency attested elsewhere in the κοινή. The papyri show that ἀλλ' ἤ could still be used in its classical sense after a negation containing a word of comparison or simply after a negative, e.g. ὀμνύω ταύτην τὴν ὑποθήκην μὴ ὑποκεῖσθαι πρὸς ἄλλο μηθὲν ἀλλ' ἢ τὴν προγεγραμμένην ἐγγύην (P. Petr. II 46 (a) 5), [2] and ὥστε μηθένα εἶναι ἐνταῦθα ἀλλ' ἢ ἡμᾶς (P. Petr. III 43 (3) 19). [3] But there are also occasions when it takes the place of ἀλλά, e.g. ξύλων ἀκαγθίνων οὐχ ὑστεροῦσι, ἀλλ' ἢ ἔχουσι ἱκανά (Zen. P. 59270, 5). [4] There are two factors which may possibly account for this development. The third category of the classical use, although explicable on the lines suggested by Denniston and J. Cook Wilson, [5] readily lends itself to a form of interpretation by which ἀλλ' ἤ comes to be regarded as the equivalent of ἀλλά. Wilson gives as an example of this form of the classical idiom the following quotation from Aristotle: εἰ δ' ἐστὶν ὁ χρόνος οὗτος τῆς κυήσεως ἢ μή ἐστιν οὐδέν πω συνῶπται μεχρί γε τοῦ νῦν, ἀλλ' ἢ ὅτι λέγεται μόνον (de Anim. Hist. 580 a 20). He comments: "The meaning is that there is nothing to go upon in the matter but hearsay; but the

---

[1] P. 26.
[2] See Mayser, p. 119.
[3] Ibid.
[4] Ibid.
[5] "On the Use of ἀλλ' ἤ in Aristotle," The Classical Quarterly, iii (1909), 121-124.

negation is expressed only for the principal source of evidence. 'We have not the evidence of searching observation: (nor indeed any evidence) but hearsay.' " Now while the contents of the ellipsis may well have been in the mind of the original writer, and may have led him to use a connective which normally introduces an exception, it would be very easy for his readers to fail to notice the existence of an ellipsis, to read ἀλλ' ἤ as though it were ἀλλά ("We have not the evidence of observation but only of hearsay"), and so themselves to come to use ἀλλ' ἤ to introduce a negation.

Secondly, it happens occasionally that ἀλλά itself is used to introduce an exception. Denniston [1] gives two examples from Aristotle: πολλῶν τε οὐσῶν αἰτιῶν . . . οὐ λέγει ἀλλὰ μίαν (Pol. 1316 b 15), and ἐν οὐδεμιᾷ τέχνῃ ἀλλ' ἐν ῥητορικῇ καὶ ἐριστικῇ (Ars Rhet. 1402 a 27). The idiom is also found in the papyri and in the New Testament; e.g. καὶ μὴ ἐξέστω Φιλίσκωι γυναῖκα ἄλλην ἐπαγάγεσθαι ἀλλὰ 'Απολλωνίαν (P. Teb. 104, 18), [2] and οὐ γάρ ἐστίν τι κρυπτόν, ἐὰν μὴ ἵνα φανερωθῇ· οὐδὲ ἐγένετο ἀπόκρυφον, ἀλλ' ἵνα ἔλθῃ εἰς φανερόν (Mk. iv 22). In connection with this second example Vincent Taylor [3] quotes Wellhausen, who thinks that ἐὰν μή and ἀλλά here correspond with the Aramaic אֶלָּא which has both exceptive and adversative meanings. This might suggest that the exceptive use of ἀλλά derives from the process of translation, and not from an idiom present in the κοινή. But in this instance it is hardly likely to be a genuine case of mistranslation due to a failure to grasp the precise function of אֶלָּא, for the same Aramaic term, used in its exceptive sense, has presumably been translated correctly by ἐὰν μή in the immediately preceding phrase, which is obviously parallel. The other possibility is that, since אֶלָּא could be translated by either term, ἐὰν μή and ἀλλά had come to be used indiscriminately for this purpose. But if they had been sharply distinguished in the κοινή this could scarcely have happened. It is more likely that Mark's use of ἀλλά here is due to the fact that ἐὰν μή and ἀλλά in the κοινή had become to some extent interchangeable expressions. It is debatable whether the exceptive use of ἀλλά begins only with Aristotle and develops in the κοινή or whether it can be regarded as a pre-Aristotelian idiom. In classical literature Denniston finds

---

[1] P. 4.
[2] See Mayser, p. 118.
[3] Vincent Taylor, *The Gospel according to St Mark*, London, 1953, p. 263.

no parallel outside Aristotle except for a single example in Sophocles, ἔπαισε δ' αὐτόχειρ νιν οὔτις ἀλλ' ἐγὼ τλάμων (*O.T.* 1331). But the fact that this example is a poetic one at least suggests the possibility, in view of the affinities between poetic and popular speech which have been pointed out by Radermacher, [1] that the idiom was all the time part of the spoken language but only emerges clearly to view in the writings of Aristotle and the documents representative of the κοινή. At any rate the existence of an exceptive use of ἀλλά at this later date is well attested, and must have assisted the process whereby ἀλλά and ἀλλ' ἤ could be virtually equated, so that ἀλλ' ἤ could be used to introduce a negation.

The use of ἀλλ' ἤ to express opposition is further attested as a κοινή idiom by the usage of the Septuagint. There are several occasions when it clearly introduces a plain contrast, rather than an exception, e.g. πλὴν σὺ οὐκ οἰκοδομήσεις τὸν οἶκον, ἀλλ' ἤ ὁ υἱός σου ὁ ἐξελθὼν ἐκ τῶν πλευρῶν σου, οὗτος οἰκοδομήσει τὸν οἶκον τῷ ὀνόματί μου (III King. viii 19), and καὶ οὐκ ἦσαν τῷ Σωσὰν υἱοί, ἀλλ' ἤ θυγατέρες (I Chron. ii 34), [2] This might be partly due to the fact that, in the verses quoted, ἀλλ' ἤ translates an original כִּי אִם. The Hebrew term, like the Aramaic אֶלָּא, may be used either to limit or to contradict the preceding clause, and so may be translated either by ἀλλ' ἤ or by ἀλλά, e.g., אֵין זֶה כִּי אִם־בֵּית אֱלֹהִים οὐκ ἔστιν τοῦτο ἀλλ' ἤ οἶκος θεοῦ (Gen. xxviii 17), and לֹא יִירָשְׁךָ זֶה כִּי־אִם אֲשֶׁר יֵצֵא מִמֵּעֶיךָ הוּא יִירָשֶׁךָ, οὐ κληρονομήσει σε οὗτος, ἀλλ' ὃς ἐξελεύσεται ἐκ σοῦ, οὗτος κληρονομήσει σε (Gen. xv 4). As in the case of the use of ἀλλά in Mk. iv 22, one must consider the possibility that the Septuagintal use of ἀλλ' ἤ to express opposition is a phenomenon which arises simply in the course of translation. But, again, the likelihood of a genuine mistake is slight. In the examples given there would seem no reason to misunderstand a negating כִּי אִם and take it as exceptive.

And if there was a tendency when translating כִּי אִם to use either particle without distinction, the original exceptive function of ἀλλ' ἤ could hardly have been defined very clearly in the κοινή. Further, there is one occasion when ἀλλ' ἤ is used as the equivalent of the simple כִּי, namely in I King. viii 7, כִּי לֹא אֹתְךָ מָאָסוּ כִּי־אֹתִי מָאֲסוּ מִמְּלֹךְ

---

[1] *Koine*, pp. 24-25.
[2] Cf. IV King. xix 18; I Chron. xxiii 22.

עֲלֵיהֶם ὅτι οὐ σὲ ἐξουθενήκασιν, ἀλλ' ἢ ἐμὲ ἐξουδενώκασιν τοῦ μὴ βασιλεύειν ἐπ' αὐτῶν. The word כִּי by itself does not possess an exceptive function, so that the use of ἀλλ' ἢ cannot here be attributed to the process of translation, but must be accounted for by the equivalence of ἀλλ' ἢ and ἀλλά in the κοινή.

b. πλήν as an Adversative and Progressive Conjunction

When πλήν is used as a conjunction in classical literature its force is limitative, "except that," "only," e.g. ὕστερον δὲ πολὺ μεταλλάξαντες τῆς τοῦ δήμου διοικήσεως (πλὴν τοὺς φεύγοντας οὐ κατῆγον τοῦ 'Αλκιβιάδου δὴ ἕνεκα) τὰ δὲ ἄλλα ἔνεμον κατὰ κράτος τὴν πόλιν (Thuc. VIII 70). [1] This classical use reappears in the literature of the Hellenistic period, e.g. ἅμα τε τὰ λείψανα μετηνέχθη καὶ τοὔνομα τῆς Ταρπηίας ἐξέλιπε· πλὴν πέτραν ἔτι νῦν ἐν τῷ Καπιτωλίῳ Ταρπηίαν καλοῦσιν (Plut. Vit. Par. I i, Rom. xviii). [2] And it is also found in various representatives of the κοινή, e.g. ἔστι δὲ παραπλησία τῷ μεγέθει καὶ τῷ σχήματι τῷ κατ' Αἴγυπτον καλουμένῳ Δέλτα, πλὴν ἐκείνου μὲν θάλαττα τὴν μίαν πλευρὰν καὶ τὰς τῶν ποταμῶν ῥύσεις ἐπιζεύγνυσι, ταύτης δ' ὄρη... (Polyb. III 49, 7); τί διαφέρει οἰκία ἀνθρώπου καὶ νεοσσιὰ πελαργοῦ ὡς οἴκησις. πλὴν ὅτι ὁ μὲν ἐκ δοκῶν καὶ κεραμίδων καὶ πλίνθων οἰκοδομεῖ τὰ οἰκίδια, ὁ δ' ἐκ ῥάβδων καὶ πηλοῦ (Epict. Dss. I 28, 17); [3] and τὰ ἐν αὐτῇ συναντήσοντα ἐμοὶ μὴ εἰδώς, πλὴν ὅτι τὸ πνεῦμα τὸ ἅγιον κατὰ πόλιν διαμαρτύρεταί μοι λέγον ὅτι δεσμὰ καὶ θλίψεις με μένουσιν (Acts xx 22-23). [4] Its occurrence in the Septuagint is likewise an indication that it continued to be employed in this period: καὶ ἐξωλεθρεύσαμεν πᾶσαν πόλιν ἑξῆς..., οὐ κατελίπομεν ζωγρείαν· πλὴν τὰ κτήνη ἐπρονομεύσαμεν... (Deut. ii 34-35) and καὶ ἡ πόλις ἐνεπρήσθη ἐμπυρισμῷ σὺν πᾶσιν τοῖς ἐν αὐτῇ, πλὴν ἀργυρίου καὶ χρυσίου καὶ χαλκοῦ καὶ σιδήρου ἔδωκαν εἰς θησαυρὸν κυρίου εἰσενεχθῆναι (Josh. vi 24). [5]

But, in addition to this exceptive use, πλήν also develops a purely adversative function, and in this sense it occurs in several of the New Testament writings. There is one clear example in Matthew, οὐαὶ τῷ κόσμῳ ἀπὸ τῶν σκανδάλων· ἀνάγκη γὰρ ἐλθεῖν τὰ σκάνδαλα· πλὴν οὐαὶ τῷ ἀνθρώπῳ, δι' οὗ τὸ σκάνδαλον ἔρχεται (Mt. xviii 7).

---

[1] Cf. Hdt. VII 32; Pl. Prt. 328 E; Xen. Anab. I viii 20.
[2] Cf. Vit. Par. III ii, Lycurg. xvi.
[3] See the Budé edition for this reading; cf. I 29, 12; II 23, 11.
[4] Cf. Rev. ii 25.
[5] Cf. Josh. vi 17; III King. iii 3.

Here πλήν acts as a balancing adversative particle, the equivalent of
δέ or μέντοι. In Luke there are several instances of πλήν used in this
way, e.g. ὅτι ὁ υἱὸς μὲν τοῦ ἀνθρώπου κατὰ τὸ ὡρισμένον πορεύεται,
πλὴν οὐαὶ τῷ ἀνθρώπῳ ἐκείνῳ δι᾽ οὗ παραδίδοται (Lk. xxii 22), and
μακάριοι οἱ πτωχοί, . . . πλὴν οὐαὶ ὑμῖν τοῖς πλουσίοις (Lk. vi 20, 24).
The other examples occur in the following verses: Lk. x 11, 20;
xiii 33; xviii 8. In all probability there is a further instance in Lk.
xvii 1, where some texts have δέ, but πλήν seems to be the preferable
reading. [1] In the Pauline Epistles there are four examples of πλήν
as a conjunction, and in three out of the four it functions as a
balancing adversative. The clearest instance is in Phil. iv 11, 14,
οὐχ ὅτι καθ᾽ ὑστέρησιν λέγω· ἐγὼ γὰρ ἔμαθον, ἐν οἷς εἰμι, αὐτάρκης
εἶναι . . . πλὴν καλῶς ἐποιήσατε συγκοινωνήσαντές μου τῇ θλίψει. The
other two occur in I Cor. xi 11 and Eph. v 33.

The comparative frequency of adversative πλήν in Luke might
possibly be attributed to the influence of the Septuagint, as Luke
shows other signs of having imitated Septuagintal style, in which
the use of πλήν in an adversative sense is not uncommon. [2] But its
occurrence in the Pauline Epistles suggests that it is an idiom which
was present also in the κοινή. And there are, in fact, examples to be
found where πλήν is used as the equivalent of δέ or μέντοι, e.g. καίτοι
νῦν ἀκούω ὅτι καὶ οἱ ἰατροὶ παρακαλοῦσιν ἐν Ῥώμῃ· πλὴν ἐπ᾽ ἐμοῦ παρε-
καλοῦντο (Epict. Dss. III 23, 27), and θαυμάζω εἴπερ ὁ ἀποστελλό-
μενος πρὸς σὲ τὸ πλοῖον τὸ τοῦ γεούχου καταλαμβάνει παρὰ σοί. πλὴν ἐὰν
διὰ ἀμελίαν τινὰ καταλάβῃ, σπούδασον πάραυτα τὸν ναύτην ἐπὶ τὴν
πόλειν ἅμα τῷ πεμφθέντι συμμάχῳ ἐκπέμψαι (P. Oxy. IX 1223). [3]

In some of the Lucan examples of adversative πλήν it is used as
the equivalent of ἀλλά, e.g. μὴ κλαίετε ἐπ᾽ ἐμέ, πλὴν ἐφ᾽ ἑαυτὰς κλαίετε
(Lk. xxiii 28), and μὴ ζητεῖτε τί φάγητε καὶ τί πίητε . . . πλὴν ζητεῖτε
τὴν βασιλείαν αὐτοῦ . . . (Lk. xii 29, 31). The other instances occur

---

[1] This is the Lucan equivalent of Mt. xviii 7. Matthew has πλήν, and
this was probably the original form of the saying, as Matthew himself uses
πλήν infrequently (there are four examples in addition to this one, two of
which seem to be derived from his source) and would not be likely to alter
an original δέ. But if πλήν was original, Luke is unlikely to have altered it in
his own version: he uses πλήν frequently, and has πλὴν οὐαί twice. Moreover,
πλήν has better manuscript attestation than δέ (πλην ουαι, BℵD it Syˢ; ουαι
δε, Θ and the Byzantine text), and could scarcely be due to Alexandrian
revision (in the sense of stylistic improvement), since δέ is the better word
from the classical standpoint.

[2] See, e.g., Deut. x 15; xviii 20; I King. xii 20; III King. xv 14.

[3] See Hunt and Edgar, op. cit., No. 164.

in Lk. vi 35; xxii 21; xxii 42. This form of adversative πλήν does not occur in the Septuagint, and the Lucan usage reflects the idiom of the κοινή, e.g. οὐδὲ γὰρ τοῦτό μοι σπουδαιότε[ρο]ν ἐξ ἁπάντω[ν] χρηματίζεσθαι, πλὴν μᾶλλον φιλανθρωπίᾳ τε καὶ εὐεργεσίαις συναύξειν ταύτην τὴν ἀρχήν (P. Fay. 20¹⁶). There is a further example in Plutarch's life of Pericles. We are told that Pericles was attacked by his enemies for not engaging in battle with the Spartans; the author then continues, πλὴν ὑπ' οὐδενὸς ἐκινήθη τῶν τοιούτων ὁ Περικλῆς . . . . (Plut. Vit. Par. I ii Per. xxxiv). [1] In Lk. xxii 21 πλήν seems to be used to indicate a break-off in the thought and a transition to a different point, καὶ λαβὼν ἄρτον εὐχαριστήσας ἔκλασεν καὶ ἔδωκεν αὐτοῖς λέγων· τοῦτό ἐστιν τὸ σῶμά μου. πλὴν ἰδοὺ ἡ χεὶρ τοῦ παραδιδόντος με μετ' ἐμοῦ ἐπὶ τῆς τραπέζης. This is a function which in classical Greek could be performed by ἀλλά, [2] so that it is probably correct to treat πλήν as the equivalent of ἀλλά here. There is a parallel example in Polybius. In his summing-up at the end of his account of the First Punic War he emphasizes the vast scale of operations and the fact that on the part of the Romans the war was the beginning of an attempt at universal supremacy. He then digresses on the subject of Roman political institutions and the incompetence of those who have previously written about them, and finally resumes his consideration of the war as follows: πλὴν ἔν γε τῷ προειρημένῳ πολέμῳ τὰς μὲν τῶν πολιτευμάτων ἀμφοτέρων προαιρέσεις ἐφαμίλλους εὕροι τις ἂν γεγενημένας, οὐ μόνον ταῖς ἐπιβολαῖς ἀλλὰ καὶ ταῖς μεγαλοψυχίαις, μάλιστα δὲ τῇ περὶ τῶν πρωτείων φιλοτιμίᾳ . . . (Polyb. I 64, 5).

There are two further examples of πλήν in Luke where its function may well be progressive rather than exceptive or adversative. In the mission charge to the Seventy Jesus reproaches the cities in which he has accomplished his works of healing, and says that the inhabitants of Tyre and Sidon, if they had seen them, would have repented. He continues, πλὴν Τύρῳ καὶ Σιδῶνι ἀνεκτότερον ἔσται ἐν τῇ κρίσει ἢ ὑμῖν (Lk. x 14). To treat πλήν as adversative here involves the assumption of an ellipsis ("they did not see them, neither did they repent"), and gives an incorrect emphasis (the saying is not concerned with the failure of Tyre and Sidon to repent). It is easier to regard it as progressive, meaning "moreover," or "and indeed." The second possible example of πλήν used in this sense is found at

---

[1] Cf. Joseph., de Bell. Jud. II 116; Herm. IV, Fr. xxv 3.

[2] See Denn., pp. 8, 16, 22. As a prose example he mentions Lys. xiii 79: ἀλλ' ἕτερον, "But there is another point."

the end of the Parable of the Pounds; the preceding verses describe the punishment of the slave who has done nothing with the money entrusted to him, and express a more general formula of condemnation, ἀπὸ δὲ τοῦ μὴ ἔχοντος καὶ ὃ ἔχει ἀρθήσεται. The parable ends with the words, πλὴν τοὺς ἐχθρούς μου τούτους . . . ἀγάγετε ὧδε καὶ κατασφάξατε αὐτοὺς ἔμπροσθέν μου (Lk. xix 27). Here πλήν could be understood as meaning "and, what is more."

There would appear, however, to be no examples of πλήν used in this way in the κοινή, and while it is not impossible that a current idiom should happen to be attested only in the New Testament, the more likely explanation is that the use derives from the Septuagint. Here πλήν is frequently used to translate the Hebrew אַךְ in its restrictive or adversative sense. [1] But the Hebrew particle also performs a purely asseverative function, meaning "surely," or "no doubt," and in this sense, too, it is translated by πλήν, e.g. אָמַרְתִּי אַךְ־תִּירְאִי אוֹתִי εἶπα πλὴν φοβεῖσθέ με . . . . (Zeph. iii 7). [2] As πλήν occurs here at the beginning of a speech it is a little difficult to determine how it would have been regarded by readers whose natural language was Greek, but it might perhaps have assumed an inceptive force, such as occasionally attached to ἀλλά. [3] In the following example, however, it could very well be understood as a progressive particle, "moreover," ἐγὼ ἀνὴρ ὁ βλέπων πτωχείαν ἐν ῥάβδῳ θυμοῦ αὐτοῦ ἐπ' ἐμέ· παρέλαβέν με καὶ ἀπήγαγεν εἰς σκότος καὶ οὐ φῶς, πλὴν ἐν ἐμοὶ ἐπέστρεψεν χεῖρα αὐτοῦ ὅλην τὴν ἡμέραν (Lam. iii 1-3). Other instances occur as follows: Ps. xxxviii 6-7; lxvii 22; cxxxix 14; Hos. xii 9; Jer. xii 1; IV King. xxiii 35; xxiv 3.

Finally, there is one occurrence of πλήν in Luke where it appears to introduce an inference: νῦν ὑμεῖς οἱ Φαρισαῖοι τὸ ἔξωθεν τοῦ ποτηρίου καὶ τοῦ πίνακος καθαρίζετε, τὸ δὲ ἔσωθεν ὑμῶν γέμει ἁρπαγῆς καὶ πονηρίας. ἄφρονες, οὐχ ὁ ποιήσας τὸ ἔξωθεν καὶ τὸ ἔσωθεν ἐποίησε; πλὴν τὰ ἐνόντα δότε ἐλεημοσύνην· καὶ ἰδού, πάντα καθαρὰ ὑμῖν ἐστιν (Lk. xi 39-41). The suggestion that πλήν can represent οὖν may seem a highly improbable one. Nevertheless there are two considerations which may be urged in its favor. First, there is an example of πλήν in the Clementine Homilies which is clearly inferential: γελᾶτε

---

[1] E.g. Gen. ix 4; Lev. xi 3-4; xxi 23; Num. xviii 3; xviii 17; xxxvi 6; Jg. x 15; II King. iii 13; III King. xxii 44; IV King. xxiii 26; Ps. xlviii 16; lxxiv 9; Jer. iii 13; x 24; xxxiii 24; xxxv 7.

[2] Cf. Jg. xx 39 (A-text).

[3] See Denn., pp. 20-21.

ὑμεῖς τὰ ἐκείνων, οὐκ εἰδότες πολλῷ μᾶλλον ὑπ' ἐκείνων γελώμενοι. πλὴν τὰ ἀλλήλων γελᾶτε (Hom. Clem. x 17). Secondly, there is some evidence to show that πλήν may occasionally have been used instead of μὲν οὖν as a particle of transition. In II Macc. vi 17 πλήν introduces a sentence which serves to conclude one topic and is followed by a δέ-clause indicating that the writer is passing on to the next point: πλὴν ἕως ὑπομνήσεως ταῦθ' ἡμῖν εἰρήσθω· δι' ὀλίγων δ' ἐλευστέον ἐπὶ τὴν διήγησιν. Here πλήν could clearly be regarded as the equivalent of μὲν οὖν, and this equivalence is supported by the fact that at the end of the seventh chapter there is a summarizing sentence introduced by μὲν οὖν which is similar in construction to the one in the sixth chapter which begins with πλήν: τὰ μὲν οὖν περὶ τοὺς σπλαγχνισμοὺς καὶ τὰς ὑπερβαλλούσας αἰκίας ἐπὶ τοσοῦτον δεδηλώσθω. Ἰουδας δὲ ὁ καὶ Μακκαβαῖος . . . . (II Macc. vii 42-viii 1). There is a further example in the first book of Polybius. The author is describing the revolt of the Carthaginian mercenaries and concludes his account of the riotous assemblies, at which the mob stoned all the speakers other than their ringleaders, Spendius and Matho, as follows: πλὴν οὐδενὸς ἔτι τολμῶντος συμβουλεύειν διὰ ταύτην τὴν αἰτίαν, κατέστησαν αὐτῶν στρατηγοὺς Μάθω καὶ Σπένδιον (Polyb. I 69, 14). In the next sentence he turns to the actions of the general sent to deal with the disturbances and begins, ὁ δὲ Γέσκων . . . . As in II Maccabees, the sense required for πλήν is that of μὲν οὖν. If πλήν had come to be used in this transitional sense, it is possible that it may further have developed a more definitely inferential force.

The development of πλήν since the classical period is one of the most interesting of the linguistic phenomena which are exhibited by the New Testament and by the other extant witnesses to the κοινή. The growth of the adversative sense is not particularly difficult to account for. An exception is also a contrast, and the alternation and equivalence of ἀλλ' ἤ and ἀλλά in Hellenistic Greek shows that the distinction between the ideas of exception on the one hand and contrast and negation on the other was not felt very strongly and that a particle which indicated the one could come to indicate the other also. One aspect of the adversative function of πλήν was its use, like that of ἀλλά, to indicate a break-off in the thought. This may have led to its employment as a transitional particle, in the sense of μὲν οὖν. Finally, if an inferential function is occasionally to be detected, this will have developed out of the transitional use.

4. *Formation of Connecting Particles from Other Parts of Speech*

Several of the classical particles are clearly derived originally from other parts of speech. Denniston points out that ἀλλά derives from ἄλλα, "other things," that τοι was the dative of the second person singular pronoun, and that που was probably "somewhere." [1] A similar process of development is visible in the κοινή.

a. (τὸ) λοιπόν

In classical Greek the neuter form of the adjective λοιπός, used without a following substantive, is employed in two different ways. In the nominative case, followed by some part of εἶναι and the infinitive of another verb, it means "it remains," e.g. τὸ δὴ λοιπὸν ἤδη ... ἡμῖν ἐστὶ σκέψασθαι. . . . (Pl. *R.* 444 E), and οὐκοῦν λοιπὸν ἂν εἴη ἡμῖν ἃ ἕκαστος ὑπέσχετο ἀποδεικνύναι ὡς πολλοῦ ἄξιά ἐστιν (Xen. *Conv.* iv 1). Secondly, in the accusative case (and also in the genitive) it is used as the equivalent of a temporal adverb and means "henceforward," "for the future," e.g. κἀγὼ 'πακούσας ταῦτα τὴν Κορινθίαν ἄστροις τὸ λοιπὸν τεκμαρούμενος χθόνα ἔφευγον (Soph. *O.T.* 794-796).

In later Greek, however, λοιπόν, with or without the definite article, becomes little more than a connecting particle used in the same way as οὖν. Jannaris maintains that it is this sense of λοιπόν, "therefore," "then," "well then," that is found in the New Testament. [2] He gives the following references, which it will be convenient to set out in full: καθεύδετε τὸ λοιπὸν καὶ ἀναπαύεσθε (Mk. xiv 41); οὕτως ἡμᾶς λογιζέσθω ἄνθρωπος ὡς ὑπηρέτας Χριστοῦ καὶ οἰκονόμους μυστηρίων θεοῦ. ὧδε λοιπὸν ζητεῖται ἐν τοῖς οἰκονόμοις ἵνα πιστός τις εὑρεθῇ (I Cor. iv 1-2); ὁ καιρὸς συνεσταλμένος ἐστίν· τὸ λοιπὸν ἵνα καὶ οἱ ἔχοντες γυναῖκας ὡς μὴ ἔχοντες ὦσιν (I Cor. vii 29); λοιπόν, ἀδελφοί, χαίρετε (II Cor. xiii 11); τὸ λοιπόν, ἀδελφοί μου, χαίρετε ἐν κυρίῳ (Phil. iii 1); τὸ λοιπόν, ἀδελφοί, ὅσα ἐστὶν ἀληθῆ, . . . ταῦτα λογίζεσθε (Phil. iv 8); . . . εἰς τὸ στηρίξαι ὑμῶν τὰς καρδίας ἀμέμπτους ἐν ἁγιωσύνῃ ἔμπροσθεν τοῦ θεοῦ καὶ πατρὸς ἡμῶν ἐν τῇ παρουσίᾳ τοῦ κυρίου ἡμῶν Ἰησοῦ μετὰ πάντων τῶν ἁγίων αὐτοῦ. λοιπὸν οὖν, ἀδελφοί, ἐρωτῶμεν ὑμᾶς . . . ἵνα καθὼς παρελάβετε παρ' ἡμῶν τὸ πῶς δεῖ ὑμᾶς περιπατεῖν καὶ ἀρέσκειν θεῷ, . . . ἵνα περισσεύητε μᾶλλον

---

[1] P. xxxvii.

[2] A. N. Jannaris, "Misreadings and Misrenderings in the New Testament," *Expositor*, Fifth Series, viii (1898), 429-431.

(I Thess. iii 13-iv 1); παρακαλέσαι ὑμῶν τὰς καρδίας καὶ στηρίξαι ἐν παντὶ ἔργῳ καὶ λόγῳ ἀγαθῷ. τὸ λοιπὸν προσεύχεσθε, ἀδελφοί, περὶ ἡμῶν (II Thess. ii 17-iii 1); and τὸν καλὸν ἀγῶνα ἠγώνισμαι, τὸν δρόμον τετέλεκα, τὴν πίστιν τετήρηκα· λοιπὸν ἀπόκειταί μοι ὁ τῆς δικαιοσύνης στέφανος, ὃν ἀποδώσει μοι ὁ κύριος ἐν ἐκείνῃ τῇ ἡμέρᾳ (II Tim. iv 7-8; Jannaris also makes reference to Eph. vi 10, but here the correct reading is more probably τοῦ λοιποῦ, which in Gal. vi 17 is temporal, "henceforth").

In some of these examples, however, different interpretations of λοιπόν may be offered. The Marcan reference is in any case obscure; if καθεύδετε is an imperative, and not part of a question, the following λοιπόν might well be temporal, and the whole phrase mean, "Go on sleeping." In II Cor. xiii 11 the term may act as a concluding epistolary formula which demands special consideration and is not to be taken as an outright equivalent for οὖν. [1] This may also be true of Phil. iii 1. Certainly it is nowhere near the actual end of the letter, but the whole phrase is similar to that in II Cor. xiii 11, and since the following sentence has no apparent connection with it, it is worth considering whether Paul may not have begun his closing greeting at this point and then have realized that he had more to say. The example in II Tim. iv 8 might be understood as temporal, "henceforth." On the other hand, this interpretation would perhaps lay too much stress on the interval between the death of the individual Christian and the *Parousia*, which is hardly the point, and an inferential sense would suit the context very well. In I Cor. vii 29, however, a temporal reference seems entirely suitable; τὸ λοιπόν would then mean "in the remaining time," i.e. "from the present moment until the *Parousia*."

In the remaining instances there is no reason for attaching a temporal force to λοιπόν, nor does it function as a closing epistolary formula, so that Jannaris's contention that it acts as the equivalent of οὖν is probably correct. In I Cor. iv 2 there are two possible interpretations; each corresponds with a function of οὖν in classical Greek and both have parallels in the New Testament itself. The preceding word ὧδε means "in that case," "on that showing", and we might understand λοιπόν as strengthening the inferential connection of thought. Both words would refer back to the previous sentence and draw a conclusion from it. There is nothing to hinder

---

[1] See below, p. 30.

the supposition that Paul is here making use of two inferential particles one after the other, since that is precisely what he does in his use of ἄρα οὖν. In that case λοιπόν is the equivalent of the classical οὖν in its most usual sense, which needs no illustration. This is the probable function of λοιπόν in II Tim. iv 8, and in I Thess. iv 1 we have it actually combined with οὖν, each particle reinforcing the other as in the combination ἄρα οὖν. In this second instance the sentence beginning with λοιπόν introduces a fresh topic, but the thought nevertheless runs on from the previous paragraph in an inferential manner, since the reference to appearing before God at the *Parousia* leads to an exhortation to increasing efforts to please God. The second way of interpreting I Cor. iv 2 would be to take λοιπόν as introducing a fresh point, "now." It is true that this causes difficulties with the preceding ὧδε, which must refer to what has gone before. But the actual sentence which ὧδε introduces is hardly the logical consequence of the preceding one; the fact that stewards in general must be trustworthy does not follow from the application of the term to the apostles. It is possible that there is some confusion between two ways of expressing the same idea, the difference being constituted by the choice, in either case, of the elements actually expressed and those left to be assumed by the reader. The alternatives would be: (a) "We are stewards of the mysteries of God. *Therefore* (ὧδε) we must be found trustworthy (since this is a necessary quality in stewards)." (b) "We are stewards of the mysteries of God. *Now* (λοιπόν) stewards must be trustworthy (and so we must be trustworthy ourselves)." Paul will have begun the sentence with the first alternative in mind and then almost immediately, with λοιπόν, have changed over to the expression of the second. Thus λοιπόν becomes an inceptive particle, looking forward, rather than an inferential connective, looking back. In classical Greek οὖν can be used in the same way, proceeding to a new point. Denniston notices the following instance in Thucydides, μία δὲ κλίνη κενὴ φέρεται ἐστρωμένη τῶν ἀφανῶν ... ξυνεκφέρει δὲ ὁ βουλόμενος καὶ ἀστῶν καὶ ξένων καὶ γυναῖκες πάρεισιν .... τιθέασιν οὖν ἐς τὸ δημόσιον σῆμα .... (Thuc. II 34). He also quotes from Hippocrates, ἐπεὶ δὲ ἔτεκεν ... αὖθις ἤλγησεν· ἔτεκεν οὖν ἄρσεν (*Epid.* ii 2. 18). [1] The other occasions in the New Testament when λοιπόν performs this

---

[1] P. 426.

function, introducing a new idea which is not connected logically with the previous sentence, are Phil. iv 8 and II Thess. iii 1.

Thus there is clear evidence in the New Testament that λοιπόν in post-classical Greek could be used simply as a transitional particle, to introduce either a logical conclusion or a fresh point in the progress of thought. The frequency of both these uses in the κοινή can be amply illustrated from the *Discourses* of Epictetus. [1] The following examples show λοιπόν as the equivalent of inferential οὖν: (Men do not practise applying their philosophy to real life) λοιπὸν ὑπὸ τῆς ἀμελετησίας προσεπισωρεύομεν ἀεί τινα καὶ προσπλάσσομεν μείζονα τῶν καθεστώτων (*Dss.* II 16, 21); and (The citharoede, singing in the theatre, does not know the proper valuation to set upon the applause or otherwise of the crowd) ἀνάγκη λοιπὸν τρέμειν καὶ ὠχριᾶν (*Dss.* II 13, 5). In the next instance the combination λοιπὸν οὖν is used in a strongly inferential sense. Epictetus is complaining that his pupils do not put into practice the philosophy he has taught them. But this is in principle possible, so that the fault must lie either with the teacher or with the pupils: λοιπὸν οὖν ἢ παρ' ἐμέ ἐστιν ἢ παρ' ὑμᾶς ἤ, ὅπερ ἀληθέστερον, παρ' ἀμφοτέρους (*Dss.* II 19, 33). Other examples of inferential λοιπόν occur in *Dss.* II 5, 16; 5, 22; IV 5, 31; cf. also Polyb. I 15, 11; 76, 8.

In other cases λοιπόν is used to introduce a fresh point; as ἕκαστον γὰρ τῶν γινομένων ὑφ' ἡμῶν ἂν μὲν ἐπὶ μηδὲν ἀναφέρωμεν, εἰκῇ ποιήσομεν . . . λοιπὸν ἡ μέν τίς ἐστι κοινὴ ἀναφορά, ἡ δ' ἰδία (*Dss.* III 23, 3-4). Further examples of this use are found in *Dss.* I 25, 15; 27, 2; II 10, 19; cf. also Ign. *ad Smyrn.* ix 1. Moulton and Milligan quote P. Oxy. I 119[13] and BGU III 846[10] in this connection (*Vocab.* under λοιπός). Cavallin [2] seems to classify this particular idiom as "interjectional." At any rate, he speaks of an interjectional function of λοιπόν in which the temporal force is often greatly weakened and the word is used simply to introduce some new section of the argument. From the New Testament he cites Phil. iii 1 and II Thess. iii 1. The first of these is perhaps part of an epistolary formula, to be considered separately, but in the second λοιπόν performs the function of introducing a new point. His other references are I Clem. lxiv; P. Oxy. XII 1480; Epict. *Dss.* II 5, 22; 14, 9; III 7, 2. The first may be a formula, as in Philippians, and the

---

[1] As Jannaris points out in his article, but he does not make any attempt to classify the various forms of the idiom which occur in the *Discourses*.

[2] Anders Cavallin, "(τὸ) λοιπόν," *Eranos*, xxxix (1941), 121-144.

meaning in the papyrus letter is somewhat obscure. Of the examples from Epictetus the second is the most apposite, since it affords the clearest illustration of the use of λοιπόν to introduce a fresh point in the argument: τὸ ἔργον τοῦ φιλοσοφοῦντος τοιοῦτόν τι φαντα-ζόμεθα. λοιπὸν ἐφεξῆς τούτῳ ζητοῦμεν, πῶς ἔσται τοῦτο. But there seems no reason to regard the word as an interjection. This is not one of the more lively sections of the *Discourses*, and when Epictetus does want the sort of effect which is achieved by the use of an interjection, he uses τί οὖν; or τί δέ; or occasionally νὴ Δία. Nor do the other examples of λοιπόν introducing a new point necessarily suggest the use of an interjection. Moreover, an interjection, by definition, has no structural function in relation to the sentence in which it occurs, but λοιπόν, by acting as a transitional particle and showing that the following sentence constitutes a fresh stage in the process of thought, does possess a structural function in relation to its context. The idea, therefore, of treating λοιπόν as an interjection would appear to be an unnecessary complication.

It remains to consider briefly the process of development which produced these uses of λοιπόν in the κοινή. Cavallin points out that it can be used to introduce the final member in a series, and quotes from a description of the Apennines in Polybius: they begin above Marseilles, and from there as far as Pisa and Arretium they are inhabited by the Ligurians; then they are inhabited by the Etrus-cans, and next by the Umbrians: λοιπὸν ὁ μὲν 'Απεννῖνος, ἀπέχων τῆς κατὰ τὸν 'Αδρίαν θαλάττης σταδίους ὡσανεὶ πεντακοσίους, ἀπολεί-πει τὰ πεδία (Polyb. II 16, 4). This use is also found in the New Testament. In the description of the shipwreck in Acts xxvii, the account of the storm ends thus: λοιπὸν περιῃρεῖτο ἐλπὶς πᾶσα τοῦ σῴζεσθαι ἡμᾶς (Acts xxvii 20). In Epictetus Cavallin notices the following example: ἐπὶ τούτοις δὲ μεμνῆσθαι, τίνες ἐσμὲν καὶ τί ἡμῖν ὄνομα, ... τίς καιρὸς ᾠδῆς, τίς καιρὸς παιδιᾶς, τίνων παρόντων· τί ἔσται ἀπὸ τοῦ πράγματος· ... πότε σκῶψαι καὶ τίνας ποτὲ καταγελάσαι καὶ ἐπὶ τίνι ποτὲ συμπεριενεχθῆναι καὶ τίνι, καὶ λοιπὸν ἐν τῇ συμπερι-φορᾷ πῶς τηρῆσαι τὸ αὐτοῦ (*Dss.* IV 12, 16-17). He appears to derive the idiom from the temporal use of λοιπόν, but he gives no definite instance of strictly temporal λοιπόν meaning "finally," "at last," and it would seem more plausible to derive it from the classical use of λοιπόν in the sense of "it remains." In the full form of this idiom, λοιπόν is followed by ἐστι and an infinitive, but the omission of ἐστι is easy enough, and occasionally the infinitive was omitted as well, as in Pl. *Phdr.* 274 B. This done, it would not be difficult to forget that λοιπόν was strictly speaking an adjective used substantivally and to treat it adverbially, meaning "lastly." In any case, it is from this use of λοιπόν to introduce the last member of a series that Cavallin would derive the inferential use; the meaning of *post hoc* passes insensibly into that of *propter hoc*. He says nothing about the origin of the second function of λοιπόν, i.e. its use to introduce a fresh point, and does not in fact distinguish the two functions very clearly. With regard to the second, there are two possibilities. λοιπόν used as a substitute for inferential οὖν might come to be employed for οὖν in general, and so develop a progressive sense. Alternatively, it sometimes introduces the last member of a series containing only two members in all, e.g. τί οὖν ἐστι τὸ παιδεύεσθαι; μανθάνειν τὰς φυσικὰς προλήψεις ἐφαρμόζειν ταῖς ἐπὶ μέρους οὐσίαις καταλλήλως τῇ φύσει καὶ λοιπὸν διελεῖν, ὅτι τῶν ὄντων τὰ μέν ἐστιν ἐφ᾽ ἡμῖν, τὰ δὲ οὐκ ἐφ᾽ ἡμῖν (Epict. *Dss.* I 22, 9-10). Here the translation "finally" would seem unnatural, and the rendering "and secondly," "and further," would be preferable.

In II Cor. xiii 11, and possibly also Phil. iii 1, where λοιπόν acts as a closing formula, it functions adverbially rather than as a transitional particle. C. F. D. Moule points out that it is the equivalent of the epistolary τὰ δ᾽ ἄλλα which introduces the final sentence in some of the papyri. [1] Now τὰ δ᾽ ἄλλα is simply an adverbial accusative of respect ("as regards the rest of what I have to say"), and λοιπόν is no doubt to be explained in the same way.

b. νῦν

Already in classical Greek there are indications that νῦν, while still retaining its function as a temporal adverb, is also developing as a non-temporal particle. There are two non-temporal uses which occur in the New Testament and the κοινή and appear to be classical in origin. The first is the use of νῦν following the imperative, e.g. ἄγε νῦν οἱ πλούσιοι, κλαύσατε . . . (Jas. v 1; cf. iv 13), and φέρε νῦν, ὦ Ζεῦ, ἣν θέλεις περίστασιν (Epict. *Dss.* I 6, 37). Liddell and Scott say that νῦν in this sense comes near to the force of the particles δή and οὖν, and they give the following examples from clas-

---

[1] C. F. D. Moule, *An Idiom Book of New Testament Greek*, Cambridge, 1953, p. 162; cf. O. Roller, *Das Formular der paulinischen Briefe*, Stuttgart, 1933, p. 66 and n. 308, who gives the following references: Witk.² nr. 53, P. Oxy. X, 1292, P. Tebt. II, 410.

sical literature: ἴθι νῦν, ἔφη ὁ Κῦρος ... (Xen. *Instit. Cyri* V iii 21), and ἄγε νῦν ἀπάρχου ... (Ar. *Pax* 1056). [1]

Secondly, νῦν δέ following a sentence expressing an unfulfilled condition is used in the sense of "but as it is," "but as the case now stands." In the New Testament this non-temporal use of νῦν δέ is rather frequent in the Fourth Gospel and occurs also in I Corinthians, e.g. εἰ μὴ ἦλθον καὶ ἐλάλησα αὐτοῖς ἁμαρτίαν οὐκ εἴχοσαν· νῦν δὲ πρόφασιν οὐκ ἔχουσιν περὶ τῆς ἁμαρτίας αὐτῶν (Jn. xv 22), [2] and εἰ δὲ ἦν τὰ πάντα ἓν μέλος ποῦ τὸ σῶμα; νῦν δὲ πολλὰ μὲν μέλη, ἓν δὲ σῶμα (I Cor. xii 19-20). [3] There are frequent instances in Epictetus, e.g. ἀλλ᾽ εἰ μὲν τὸ ἄγαλμα ἦς τὸ Φειδίου, ἡ ᾽Αθηνᾶ ἢ ὁ Ζεύς, ἐμέμνησο ἂν καὶ σαυτοῦ καὶ τοῦ τεχνίτου καὶ εἴ τινα αἴσθησιν εἶχες, ἐπειρῶ ἂν μηδὲν ἀνάξιον ποιεῖν τοῦ κατασκευάσαντος μηδὲ σεαυτοῦ, μηδ᾽ ἐν ἀπρεπεῖ σχήματι φαίνεσθαι τοῖς ὁρῶσι· νῦν δέ σε ὅτι ὁ Ζεὺς πεποίηκεν, διὰ τοῦτο ἀμελεῖς οἷόν τινα δείξεις σεαυτόν; (*Dss.* II 8, 18-19). [4] In classical Greek this idiom is used by Thucydides, e.g. ἐνθυμώμεθα δὲ καὶ ὅτι εἰ μὲν ἡμῶν ἦσαν ἑκάστοις πρὸς ἀντιπάλους περὶ γῆς ὅρων αἱ διαφοραί, οἰστὸν ἂν ἦν· νῦν δὲ πρὸς ξύμπαντάς τε ἡμᾶς ᾽Αθηναῖοι ἱκανοὶ καὶ κατὰ πόλιν ἔτι δυνατώτεροι .... (Thuc. I 122). [5]

It is possible that in the κοινή the non-temporal function of νῦν has developed further. In the New Testament there are occasions when νῦν, καὶ νῦν, and νῦν οὖν have lost their temporal force and the original temporal adverb acts simply as a connective of one sort or another. In the case of καὶ νῦν and νῦν οὖν the possibility of derivation from the Septuagint must be taken into consideration, but as there is in Epictetus a parallel to each of the three non-temporal uses, one may tentatively suggest that the idiom was secular as well as Biblical.

There is one example in Luke and one in Epictetus where νῦν, in each case followed by a pronoun, appears to exercise a purely inceptive function, in the same way as the English "now": εἶπεν δὲ ὁ κύριος πρὸς αὐτόν· νῦν ὑμεῖς οἱ Φαρισαῖοι τὸ ἔξωθεν τοῦ ποτηρίου καὶ τοῦ πίνακος καθαρίζετε .... (Lk. xi 39), and οὕτως καὶ ἐχυρὰν πόλιν οἱ οἰκοῦντες καταγελῶσι τῶν πολιορκούντων· νῦν οὗτοι τί πρᾶγμα ἔχουσιν ἐπὶ τῷ μηδενί; (Epict. *Dss.* IV 5, 25). Has this use developed

---

[1] Cf. *Pl.* 789; *V.* 381.
[2] Cf. also viii 40; ix 41; xv 24; xviii 36.
[3] Cf. also vii 14; xii 18; Heb. xi 16; νυνὶ δέ in I Cor. xv 20; Heb. ix 26.
[4] Cf. also I 1, 11; 3, 3; 26, 16; II 1, 4; 7, 12; 8, 6; 8, 19; 10, 6; 16, 20; 18, 26; III 19, 4; IV 3, 10; 8, 13; 13, 18.
[5] Cf. also III 113; IV 126; Pl. *Cra.* 384 B.

from the use of νῦν after imperatives such as ἄγε and φέρε? These
are little more than devices for attracting attention; their significance lies not in the literal sense of the verb but in the fact that
they serve as an introduction to some point which requires emphasis.
If the strict meaning of the verb is inessential to the function of
the phrase, it is possible that the verb itself may on occasion have
dropped out, and that νῦν may have performed in isolation the
same function which it performs in combination with the imperatives. There is one interesting example of νῦν in the Septuagint
which may perhaps confirm this hypothesis. In Gen. xviii 27 it is
used to translate the Hebrew הִנֵּה־נָא. Although the tone of the
Hebrew particles is rather different from that of the Greek phrases
such as ἄγε νῦν, being more deferential, nevertheless they serve as
an emphatic introduction to the following sentence in much the
same way as does the Greek idiom. The implication is that νῦν by
itself could perform the same function. Otherwise, there would
be no reason for its use here, since it is not in any way a natural
rendering of the Hebrew, such as would automatically suggest
itself to a translator. Further confirmation may possibly be found in
the fact that in the Lucan example νῦν is followed by a vocative
in the same way as are the two occurrences of ἄγε νῦν in James.

A second and slightly different development of the classical use
of νῦν following an imperative is to be seen in the use of καὶ νῦν in
an inferential sense, "and so." Since νῦν in the classical idiom acts as
the equivalent of οὖν, the transition is an easy one, and is in fact
nothing more than a change in the position of νῦν and the addition
of a further connective. In two of the examples from the New
Testament and in the example from Epictetus καὶ νῦν is used with an
imperative in the same way as the classical νῦν: καὶ νῦν πέμψον . . . .
(Acts x 5), καὶ νῦν, τεκνία, μένετε ἐν αὐτῷ (I Jn. ii 28), and εἰ δ' ἵππον
σοι πεπιστεύκει ἡ φύσις, περιεώρας αὐτὸν καὶ ἀτημέλητον; καὶ νῦν
οἴου σου τὸ σῶμα ὡς ἵππον ἐγκεχειρίσθαι (Epict. Dss. IV 11, 17).
In a second example from Acts an imperative follows καὶ νῦν at no
great distance: καὶ νῦν τί μέλλεις; ἀναστὰς βάπτισαι . . . . (Acts
xxii 16). It is possible that in Acts the use of καὶ νῦν followed by
an imperative may be derived from the Septuagint, where it occurs
with some frequency, e.g. Exod. xxxii 32; I King. ix 13; x 19; xv 1,
25; xxiv 22; xxv 17. In the Septuagint its use is due to the fact that
it is a literal translation of וְעַתָּה and its inferential force corresponds
to the use of the Hebrew particles for the purpose of drawing a

conclusion. Thus the Septuagint provides no evidence of the inferential use of καὶ νῦν in the κοινή, and the same may be true of Acts. But since there is one instance in Epictetus, and since, also, it occurs in I John, where the style in general remains uninfluenced by the Septuagint, there may be some justification for regarding the idiom as part of the common speech.

There are two occasions in Acts when the combination νῦν οὖν seems to be lacking in any definite temporal force and is probably to be understood as simply inferential: ἀπέσταλκαν οἱ στρατηγοὶ ἵνα ἀπολυθῆτε. νῦν οὖν ἐξελθόντες πορεύεσθε ἐν εἰρήνῃ (Acts xvi 36), and ἀναθέματι ἀνεθεματίσαμεν ἑαυτοὺς μηδενὸς γεύσασθαι ἕως οὗ ἀποκτείνωμεν τὸν Παῦλον. νῦν οὖν ὑμεῖς ἐμφανίσατε τῷ χιλιάρχῳ σὺν τῷ συνεδρίῳ ὅπως καταγάγῃ αὐτὸν εἰς ὑμᾶς ὡς μέλλοντας διαγινώσκειν ἀκριβέστερον τὰ περὶ αὐτοῦ (Acts xxiii 14-15). The Bauer-Arndt-Gingrich lexicon gives Acts xv 10 as a further example of this use of νῦν οὖν, but here a temporal sense is possible for νῦν, as there may be a contrast with ἀφ' ἡμερῶν ἀρχαίων in verse 7. In the Septuagint there are several instances of inferential νῦν οὖν in Genesis, e.g. ἀπέστειλεν γάρ με ὁ θεὸς ἔμπροσθεν ὑμῶν, ὑπολείπεσθαι ὑμῶν κατάλειμμα ἐπὶ τῆς γῆς καὶ ἐκθρέψαι ὑμῶν κατάλειψιν μεγάλην. νῦν οὖν οὐχ ὑμεῖς με ἀπεστάλκατε ὧδε, ἀλλ' ἢ ὁ θεός (Gen. xlv 7-8); compare also Gen. xxvii 8, 43; xxxi 16, 30, 44; xxxvii 20; xli 33; xliv 30, 33; xlv 5; xlvii 4. In all these examples νῦν οὖν translates an inferential וְעַתָּה. But it is clearly not a strictly literal translation, in contrast with καὶ νῦν. Therefore its appearance in the Septuagint is not due solely to the internal exigencies of translation, but may also indicate the external existence of the combination in the κοινή. Thus, while the usage of Acts is in all probability dependent upon that of the Septuagint and so is not in itself a witness to the colloquial idiom, it can in fact be treated as such because the Septuagintal phrase may itself be derived from the popular speech. Additional evidence for the existence of non-temporal νῦν οὖν in the κοινή is found in Epictetus: (One of his acquaintances swears that when he returns to Rome from exile he will lead a retired life) νῦν οὖν τί ἐποίησεν; πρὶν ἐλθεῖν εἰς τὴν Ῥώμην, ἀπήντησαν αὐτῷ παρὰ Καίσαρος πινακίδες· ὁ δὲ λαβὼν πάντων ἐκείνων ἐξελάθετο .... (Dss. I 10, 5). The Loeb edition of the Discourses here translates νῦν οὖν as "well, now." It does not introduce a consequence but rather marks the transition from the first to the second part of the story. This, however, is one of the functions of οὖν in isolation, and may have been assumed by the combination νῦν οὖν just as the same combination performs the function of inferential οὖν.

The Bauer-Arndt-Gingrich lexicon derives inferential νῦν οὖν from νῦν meaning "as things now stand," as in the classical νῦν δέ, and this derivation is suggested for inferential καὶ νῦν as well. It has been argued above that the origin of καὶ νῦν may be found in the other classical use of non-temporal νῦν, i.e. νῦν following an imperative. Both tendencies were possibly at work at the same time, and coalesced, producing the general use of νῦν as the equivalent of inferential οὖν. Its function may then have been extended so that in the combination νῦν οὖν, as in Epictetus, it becomes the equivalent of οὖν in a purely progressive sense.

5. *Change in position*

By "change in position" is meant changes in the position of particles in relation to the sentence as a whole, and also, in the case of some combinations, changes in the position of particles in relation to each other.

a. μενοῦν

In classical Greek the combination μὲν οὖν is used both connectively, as a particle of transition, and adverbially, chiefly in answers in dialogue. It is never the first word in the sentence. In the New Testament, connective μὲν οὖν remains in its classical form, but adverbial μὲν οὖν in answers has undergone two changes: the two particles are now written as one word, μενοῦν, and it has moved to the beginning of the sentence. There are three examples: ἐγένετο δὲ ἐν τῷ λέγειν αὐτὸν ταῦτα ἐπάρασά τις φωνὴν γυνὴ ἐκ τοῦ ὄχλου εἶπεν αὐτῷ· μακαρία ἡ κοιλία ἡ βαστάσασά σε καὶ μαστοὶ οὓς ἐθήλασας. αὐτὸς δὲ εἶπεν· μενοῦν μακάριοι οἱ ἀκούοντες τὸν λόγον τοῦ θεοῦ καὶ φυλάσσοντες (Lk. xi 27-28), τί ἔτι μέμφεται; τῷ γὰρ βουλήματι αὐτοῦ τίς ἀνθέστηκεν; ὦ ἄνθρωπε, μενοῦν γε σὺ τίς εἶ ὁ ἀνταποκρινόμενος τῷ θεῷ; (Rom. ix 19-20), and ἀλλὰ λέγω, μὴ οὐκ ἤκουσαν; μενοῦν γε· εἰς πᾶσαν τὴν γῆν ἐξῆλθεν ὁ φθόγγος αὐτῶν (Rom. x 18). (In Rom. ix 20 the initial vocative may be left out of account when considering the position of μενοῦν in the sentence. μενοῦν γε modifies the following words, and is unrelated to the preceding ὦ ἄνθρωπε). In the Pauline examples a third change from the classical idiom has occurred, and μενοῦν is further emphasized by γε.

Despite the alteration in position, in two out of the three instances, at any rate, the meaning of μενοῦν remains that of the classical idiom. In the second example from Romans it plainly expresses contradiction, as in the following quotation from Plato, given by Denniston [1] to illustrate the use of οὖν to emphasize adversative μέν: ἦ σὺ οὐδὲν ἡγεῖ πράττειν τὸν γραμματιστήν . . .; — ἔγωγε ἡγοῦμαι μὲν οὖν, ἔφη (Pl. *Chrm.* 161 D).

The meaning of the Lucan example is less easy to determine, as the precise significance of the saying is not very clear from the context, and all three classical functions of adverbial μὲν οὖν [2] could be attributed to the particle here without any great difficulty. It might be strictly adversative, as in Romans: "On the contrary, this parental relationship is not in itself of any importance whatsoever. The people who are blessed are those who hear the word of God and keep it." Or it might be assentient in the full sense: "Yes, certainly my mother is blessed, for the people who are blessed are those . . ." (cf. i 38). Finally, it might be corrective: "What you have said is true as far as it goes. But the blessedness of Mary does not consist simply in the fact of her relationship towards myself but in the fact that she shares in the blessedness of those who hear the word of God and keep it, and it is in this that true blessedness lies." The first two possibilities can perhaps be eliminated, however, on the grounds that when Luke wishes to express contradiction he uses elsewhere the phrase οὐχί, λέγω ὑμῖν (ἀλλ' ἤ), as in xii 51; xiii 3, 5; and when he expresses affirmation he tends to use the particle ναί, as in vii 26; x 21; xi 51; xii 5. This leaves us with μενοῦν as a corrective, "rather," as in Plato, e.g. εἰς σμικρόν γ', ἔφη, χρόνον εἴρηκας; εἰς οὐδὲν μὲν οὖν, ἔφην, ὥς γε πρὸς τὸν ἅπαντα (Pl. *R.* 498 D).

The other New Testament example does not seem to fit very happily into any of the three classical categories. Although the relation between question and answer in Rom. ix 19-20 is in a sense sharply adversative, the answer is not the sort of straightforward negation which is normally the context of adversative μὲν οὖν in classical literature. It would perhaps be easier to regard μενοῦν γε here as simply emphatic in a completely general sense, as in Phil. iii 8, and as modifying the following σύ. This perhaps constitutes a further post-classical development of adverbial μὲν οὖν, but it may, on the other hand, be peculiar to Paul.

The alteration in the position of adverbial μὲν οὖν is directly

[1] P. 475.
[2] See Denn., pp. 475-478.

attested only by the examples already quoted from the New Testament. But there are several considerations which suggest that the usage of the New Testament may be in this respect genuinely representative of the idiom of the κοινή. The use in question is independently attested by two different writers. Also, there is no possibility that they derived the idiom from the Septuagint. Thirdly, the initial position of μὲν οὖν in the sentence is condemned by Phrynichus: μὲν οὖν τοῦτο πράξω· τίς ἀνάσχοιτο οὕτω συντάττοντός τινος ἐν ἀρχῇ λόγου τὸ μὲν οὖν; οἱ γὰρ δόκιμοι ὑποτάσσουσιν, ἐγὼ μὲν οὖν λέγοντες, τὰ καλὰ μὲν οὖν καὶ τὰ μὲν οὖν πράγματα (Ecl. cccxxii). This is sufficient to show that the initial position was to some extent generally current in the common speech.

b. ἄρα

In classical literature ἄρα is used as an inferential connecting particle at the beginning of a sentence and also, occasionally, at the beginning of an apodosis. In both cases it is usually the second word, but may sometimes be postponed to a later position. [1] In the New Testament, however, it occurs several times as the first word both at the beginning of a sentence and at the beginning of an apodosis, e.g. ἄρα ἡ πίστις ἐξ ἀκοῆς (Rom. x 17; see also Mt. vii 20, xvii 26; Lk. xi 48; Acts xi 18; I Cor. xv 18; II Cor. v 15; vii 12; Gal. v 11; Heb. iv 9); εἰ γὰρ διὰ νόμου δικαιοσύνη, ἄρα Χριστὸς δωρεὰν ἀπέθανεν (Gal. ii 21); see also: Mt. xii 28; Lk. xi 20; Gal. iii 29; Heb. xii 8). There is one example in the *Hermetica* of the use of inferential ἄρα at the beginning of a sentence: ὁ δὲ ἄνθρωπος οὐκ ἔστιν ἀεί· ἄρα οὐδὲ ἀληθές ἐστι (*Herm.* III (Budé) Fr. ii A, 12). There are also a few examples of ἄρα at the beginning of an apodosis: ἂν δὲ τρέμων καὶ πενθῶν ζητῇς ἀπερίπτωτος εἶναι, ἄρα πῶς προκόπτεις; (Epict. *Dss.* I 4, 12), and ὅταν γὰρ μηδεμία ἔρις ἐνήρεισται ἐν ὑμῖν ἡ δυναμένη ὑμᾶς βασανίσαι, ἄρα κατὰ θεὸν ζῆτε (Ign. *ad Eph.* viii 1; cf. Barn. vi 19). The external evidence for the initial position of ἄρα would not appear to be extensive. But the fact that it is found in several different writers in the New Testament may indicate that it was a commoner feature of the κοινή than the external evidence suggests.

c. ἀλλά γε, καί γε, καίτοι γε

Classical Greek frequently uses γε following the particles ἀλλά, καί,

---

[1] See Denn., pp. 40-41.

and καίτοι, but almost invariably they are separated by one or more intervening words. Denniston gives one example of ἀλλά γε from a fragment of Gorgias, and a few other instances where the text is uncertain. [1] For καί γε he quotes Hippocrates: ἀμβλύνουσι γὰρ αἱ δυνάμεις ἐν ταῖς μύξῃσι καί γε ὁ θάνατος διὰ τὴν μοίρην ἔλαχεν (Septim. 9). He remarks, however, that this is insufficient to guarantee καί γε as a classical form. The form καίτοι γε is rather better attested, although it is not frequent. There are two certain occurrences in Plato: καίτοι γε ὀφειλόμενόν πού ἐστιν τοῦτο ὃ παρακατέθετο (Pl. R. 332 A), and καίτοι γ' ἐν τῇ ἡμετέρᾳ πόλει . . . . (ibid. 440 D). [2] It is worth noticing that the classical use of μέντοι is closely similar. It is often emphasized by γε, but the particles are not very frequently juxtaposed. There are, however, a few instances of this, e.g. φωνήεντα μὲν οὔ, οὐ μέντοι γε ἄφθογγα (Pl. Cra. 424 C). [3]

In the New Testament there are several examples of this kind of juxtaposition: εἰ ἄλλοις οὐκ εἰμὶ ἀπόστολος, ἀλλά γε ὑμῖν εἰμι (I Cor. ix 2), καί γε ἐπὶ τοὺς δούλους μου καὶ ἐπὶ τὰς δούλας μου . . . ἐκχεῶ ἀπὸ τοῦ πνεύματός μου (Acts ii 18), καί γε οὐκ ἀμάρτυρον αὐτὸν ἀφῆκεν (Acts xiv 17), [4] ζητεῖν τὸν θεόν . . . καί γε οὐ μακρὰν ἀπὸ ἑνὸς ἑκάστου ἡμῶν ὑπάρχοντα (Acts xvii 27), and καίτοι γε Ἰησοῦς αὐτὸς οὐκ ἐβάπτιζεν ἀλλ' οἱ μαθηταὶ αὐτοῦ (Jn. iv 2).

The transposition of γε so that it immediately follows καίτοι appears to have been fairly frequent in the Greek of the Hellenistic period. It occurs in writers typical of the κοινή, e.g. καίτοι γε προφανῶς ὁ μὲν τὸν κλέπτην ἢ μοιχὸν ἀποκτείνας ἀθῷός ἐστιν (Polyb. II 56, 15; see also 58, 14; 61, 7; Epict. Dss. III 24, 90; Diod. Sic. II v 7). But it is likewise found in Philo, who writes in a more classical style: de Agr. xiv; de Post. Caini xlviii. The same thing happens with μέντοι. The juxtaposition of μέντοι and γε is found as follows: Polyb. I 4, 11; III 12, 2; Diod. Sic. II xv 2; xxxi 8. The combination ἀλλά γε, on the other hand, seems to have very little external attestation, although there is one example in Polybius. [5] Finally, the juxtaposition of καί and γε, while clearly not as common

---

[1] P. 23. For the Gorgias quotation see above, p. 13.

[2] See Denn., p. 564. He gives as further references Xen. Mem. I ii 3; IV ii 7; Ar. Ach. 611; Nu. 876.

[3] Further examples include Pl. R. 329 E; Xen. HG. II iv 42; Instit. Cyri V v 11, 24; Ar. Th. 709.

[4] There are textual variants. For a justification of the reading καί γε, see Appendix, B.

[5] See above, p. 13 n. 2.

as either καίτοι γε or μέντοι γε, is attested by several examples: καί γε τούτου, φίλτατε, ἀπρὶξ ἐχώμεθα τοῦ σκοποῦ (Longin. de Sublim. xiii 2), τὴν μὲν παρ' ὑμῶν τιμὴν ἀσπάζομαι, καί γε ἐπὶ τούτῳ σφόδρα χαίρω (P. Oxy. I 41), καί γε πολλά, φησίν, ἔστιν (Hermas, Mand. viii 5), and καὶ πολλοὺς ἐκριζοῖ ἀπὸ τῆς πίστεως καί γε λίαν πιστοὺς καὶ ἰσχυρούς (ibid. ix 9). The use of this idiom in the secular κοινή may have been only occasional. But it is comparatively frequent in the Septuagint, from which the author of Acts may have derived it. The following references are merely a selection: Jg. ii 17; xix 19; II King. xi 12, 17, 24; xiv 6; xv 20; xvii 16; III King. i 48; IV King. xiii 6.

The evidence of the New Testament and of the secular κοινή is thus sufficient to show that there was a general tendency to place γε immediately after the particles with which it was combined, instead of allowing one word or more to intervene as in the classical idiom. Radermacher suggests that this was due to a tendency to avoid hiatus. [1] This explanation might certainly hold good for the examples quoted from the New Testament, and it may well be partly the reason for the frequency of καί γε in the Septuagint. Here it is often used for גַּם or וְגַם, and the Hebrew particle is frequently followed by pronouns such as require to be translated by αὐτός, οὗτος, or ἐγώ. It is the καί which is the primary equivalent of גַּם (meaning "also", or "even"), [2] and the γε simply emphasizes; i.e., the reason for the coherence of γε with καί is not that καί is the equivalent of וְ and γε the equivalent of גַּם and that they are juxtaposed because of the close coherence of the Hebrew particles. This being so, the reason for writing καί γε αὐτοί (Josh. ix 4) rather than καὶ αὐτοί γε, and καί γε ἐγώ (Jg. i 3 A; II King. ii 6; xviii 2) for καὶ ἔγωγε may perhaps be the desire to avoid the hiatus which would result from the juxtaposition of καί and the pronoun.

But the avoidance of hiatus is hardly sufficient to account fully for the tendency. It does not explain some of the examples already quoted, where no hiatus would occur even if γε were to be postponed to its classical position. Further, the classical combination ἀλλ' οὖν ... γέ has become ἀλλ' οὖν γε in Diodorus Siculus and Philo (Diod. Sic. I xc 4; Philo, de Virt. xl), and there is also one occasion

---

[1] Gramm., p. 35.

[2] καί γε is used for גַּם when not preceded by וְ, and γε by itself is never used as the rendering for גַּם.

in Diodorus where ἀλλὰ μὴν . . . γε has become ἀλλὰ μήν γε (I lxxxiv 2), and with these combinations there is no question of the necessity to avoid hiatus. There may have been a different tendency at work here. The evidence of the New Testament and of the papyri [1] shows that the use of γε as a separate particle had very much declined in the κοινή. As a result of this decline it may have come to be more firmly attached to the combinations of which it formed a part.

C. Conclusions

The evidence set forth in the pages above makes it clear that the use of particles in the κοινή differed in several respects from that of the classical authors. In part the difference may be regarded as a sign of linguistic degeneration. The absence from the κοινή of many of the classical combinations of particles is the most significant example of this process, and may well be a symptom of the more general decline of the classical Greek civilization. Perhaps a further example is the change in the position of γε following ἀλλά, καί, καίτοι, and μέντοι. The impression produced by the alteration is that of a loss in subtlety of expression, although this judgment is a somewhat subjective one and can hardly be established by any concrete evidence. But the change of idiom is due also to more positive processes of linguistic development. The tendency of particles gradually to develop new functions is one which is visible in the Greek of the classical period; e.g. ἀλλά develops a progressive sense which is at first sight a complete contradiction of its original adversative function; and adverbial ἄρα becomes an inferential connective in the later classical prose, as is true also of δή. This change may be regarded as a sign more of linguistic growth than of decay. It is in this light that one should view the development in the κοινή of πλήν as an adversative and transitional particle. Another process which is an indication of linguistic growth is the formation of particles from other elements of speech, and this is illustrated in the Hellenistic period by the use of λοιπόν and νῦν as particles of connection.

The New Testament provides a focus for all these processes and shows itself a reliable representative of κοινή Greek. Since this is so, it may be worthwhile, in conclusion, to draw attention

---

[1] See Mayser, p. 123.

to the two uses which appear to be illustrated by the New Testament alone: the reinforcement of progressive ἀλλὰ καί by particles of emphasis and the use of μενοῦν in the initial position in answers. Despite their lack of attestation elsewhere, the general usage of the New Testament provides some justification for their recognition as genuine idioms of the κοινή.

PART TWO

EXEGETICAL PROBLEMS INVOLVING GREEK PARTICLES IN THE NEW TESTAMENT

The exegetical problems which need examination fall into two groups. First, there are the claims put forward by several scholars that the use of some one particle by a New Testament writer possesses throughout his work a significance beyond that which attaches to it by virtue of its purely linguistic function. The interest here seems to be concentrated on the Gospel according to Mark. C. H. Bird maintains that Mark often uses γάρ to draw attention to a hidden allusion to the Old Testament. C. H. Turner claims that when δέ is used at the beginning of a paragraph it signifies a major turning-point in the narrative, and Max Zerwick suggests that the use of δέ is frequently conditioned by psychological rather than linguistic considerations. The second group of problems is concerned simply with the interpretation of several individual occurrences and the light thrown by them upon the total meaning of the passages in which they are found.

A. Hypotheses Regarding Usage

All the three theories which are concerned with the Marcan use of γάρ and δέ require to be carefully tested by means of strictly linguistic criteria. The hypotheses suggested by Bird and Zerwick can be justified and maintained only if the occurrences of γάρ and δέ upon which they depend are incapable of explanation from the linguistic point of view. Turner's theory differs slightly from the other two, in that the function which he postulates for δέ is much more closely connected with its ordinary grammatical force. Here too, however, there are certain criticisms to be made both on linguistic and on textual grounds.

1. Γάρ-*Clauses in Mark*

C. H. Bird [1] maintains that it is a characteristic of at least some of the γάρ-clauses in Mark that "either they can hardly be said to explain the preceding sentence or else they obscure rather than

---

[1] "Some γάρ Clauses in St Mark's Gospel," *Journal of Theological Studies*, n.s., iv (1953), 171-187.

illuminate the immediate context by drawing attention to some factor which is an embarrassment rather than an aid to interpretation. Commentators have found it hard to expound in what way the age of Jairus's daughter explains the fact that she immediately arose and began to walk about: or to suggest a motive for the cursing of a barren fig-tree when it was not the season of figs." He then goes on to suggest that γάρ may on occasion be used in an assertive sense, and may draw attention to a fact which is relevant to the understanding of the context although it may not directly explain the preceding sentence. In such cases the force of the particle would best be expressed in English by some such phrase as: "and the significant thing about it is . . ." This use of γάρ can be employed to emphasize one factor in a given situation which constitutes "the point of contact with another set of ideas, already familiar to the reader," which would elucidate the fuller significance of the whole context. That Mark uses γάρ in this way is indicated by the fact that it is employed as an introductory particle where Christ alludes to the Old Testament without making an explicit quotation and by means of the allusion recalls a Biblical passage or idea relevant to the immediate situation. It is possible, therefore, that some of the other γάρ-clauses in the Gospel, in cases where they are not obviously explanatory of the preceding sentence, may be intended "to invite us to take a back glance at the Old Testament that we might better understand the divine economy manifested in the events of the historical ministry of Jesus Christ." Various examples are then examined in detail, and suggestions made concerning their possible background in the Old Testament: Mk. i 16 designates Peter and Andrew as the fishermen of Ezek. xlvii, and this same chapter is also the background to Mk. xi 13 (the trees on the banks of the river bear fruit continuously); Mk. v 42 indicates that Jairus's daughter is symbolic of the New Israel coming to life.

There are, however, serious objections to this theory. The following criticism is not an attempt wholly to disprove the possibility that Old Testament symbolism may be found in Mark in places where its existence is not immediately obvious, but is intended as a demonstration that the method by which Bird attempts to detect symbolism of this kind is in fact invalid. His argument derives from three linguistic propositions: first, that γάρ possesses an assertive function; secondly, that it is this assertive use which is actually employed in Mark when γάρ introduces clear allusions to the Old Testament; thirdly, that several other occurrences of γάρ cannot be regarded as simply explanatory. The first two propositions are held to explain the third, and the exegetical conclusion which follows is that a closer investigation of the occurrence of γάρ throughout the Gospel may in itself lead to the detection of hidden allusions to the Old Testament. All three propositions, however, are of doubtful validity.

The existence of a separate asseverative use of γάρ is somewhat questionable. Denniston allows that this may have been the original function of the particle, but maintains that in extant Greek literature γάρ is probably asseverative only in combination with other particles (e.g. τοιγάρ, τοιγαροῦν) and perhaps in wishes introduced by εἰ γάρ. [1] The case for a non-explanatory use of γάρ is strongest when it occurs in questions. In most examples of this kind, however, Denniston would freely assume ellipsis where necessary, and says that there is no reason to doubt that γάρ in questions means "for." [2] But he does go on to suggest that a progressive use in questions may arise out of the normal explanatory use in supplementary questions. Owing to the frequency with which such questions are requests for explanation, γάρ comes to be regarded as the normal and obvious introductory particle. Its established connection with questions is then a stronger factor than its real explanatory significance. The explanatory sense is forgotten, and it is used in questions purely as a particle of transition. [3] Thus there is some justification for postulating the existence of at least one non-explanatory use of γάρ.

On the other hand, however, these considerations offer little or no support to the theory adduced by Bird. For one thing, this usage is confined to questions, whereas Bird's examples occur in narrative, with the exception of Mk. x 45 which is a saying of a non-interrogative character. Further, it is transitional rather than asseverative, and would approximate in function to οὖν rather than to an adverbial particle of emphasis. Bird claims, however, that there are several examples in the New Testament itself of γάρ used in the sense which he terms "assertive." For this statement he gives no references whatsoever, but as he alludes to the Grimm-

[1] P. 57.
[2] P. 80.
[3] P. 85.

Thayer lexicon it is to be presumed that he is dependent upon the examples given there. Although there seems little classical warrant for his linguistic theory, it is just possible that later Greek may provide some evidence in its favor, and it will therefore prove useful to check the references which the lexicon gives to see whether evidence of this kind is forthcoming. For γάρ meaning "assuredly" the following examples are suggested: Mt. ix 5; xvi 26; xxiii 17, 19; xxvii 23; Lk. ix 25; Jn. vii 41; Acts viii 31; xix 35; I Cor. xi 22; Phil. i 18; Jn. ix 30; Acts xvi 37; I Cor. viii 11. Of these, all except the last three are found in questions, and so can be regarded as explanatory or progressive in accordance with Denniston's classification of the functions of γάρ. They provide no support for the theory of a general and asseverative, non-explanatory use. As far as the rest of the examples are concerned, in I Cor. viii 11 γάρ can be interpreted as explanatory if it refers back to verse 9 rather than to the immediately preceding sentence, [1] and in Jn. ix 30 it perhaps reinforces implied assent [2] to the accusation in verse 28, σὺ μαθητὴς εἶ ἐκείνου ("Yes, I am, for this is the marvel, that you, the disciples of Moses, don't know this man's origin and accord him no recognition, and yet he opened my eyes"). It is only in Acts xvi 37 that an affirmative sense for γάρ seems the only possible one: καὶ νῦν λάθρα ἡμᾶς ἐκβάλλουσιν; οὐ γάρ, ἀλλὰ ἐλθόντες αὐτοὶ ἡμᾶς ἐξαγαγέτωσαν. Denniston quotes a similar occurrence in the *Lysistrata*: ἆρ' οὐ παρεῖναι τὰς γυναῖκας δῆτ' ἐχρῆν; οὐ γὰρ μὰ Δί' ἀλλὰ πετομένας ἥκειν πάλαι (Ar. *Lys.* 54-55). He comments: "ἆρ' οὐ expects an affirmative answer: it gets a negative answer, which rejects the expected affirmative in favour of a stronger one." [3] This is the only example which he gives of γάρ reinforcing an expressed negative answer. He treats it as a development of assentient γάρ in answers, which he would regard as one aspect of the particle's causal function. [4] It must be admitted that at this point the theory that γάρ, except in combinations and wishes, is always causal or explanatory appears to break down. Assentient γάρ in answers, although originating in the causal use, is to all intents and purposes simply a particle of affirmation. To this extent an asseverative

---

[1] See Denn., p. 63, for γάρ referring to a remoter context, and p. 64, for γάρ used twice with the same reference.

[2] See Denn., p. 73.

[3] P. 88.

[4] Pp. 86-88, 57.

use may be allowed to exist. But there is no reason to suppose that it occurred anywhere except in answers to questions. There is therefore no support here for Bird's theory of asseverative γάρ in Mark, since none of the examples he deals with occurs in an answer. Nor is the newer Bauer-Arndt-Gingrich lexicon of any assistance in providing more convincing examples of an affirmatory use which would substantiate Bird's hypothesis. They recognize the use in question, but apart from Acts xvi 37 the only instances they give may well be interpreted as explanatory. In I Pet. iv 15, γάρ is explanatory of the preceding ἐν ὀνόματι Χριστοῦ, as verse 16 shows; in Jas. i 7 we have the second of two successive uses of explanatory γάρ with the same reference; [1] finally, in Heb. xii 3 the γάρ-clause may provide the motive for the writer's previous sentence ("I say this because I want you to consider . . ., so that you may not grow weary . . ."). [2]

Briefly to sum up the argument thus far, it appears that the asseverative function of γάρ is strictly limited, and that the only three occasions of its use are the combinations of γάρ with other particles, wishes introduced by εἰ γάρ, and answers to questions. Neither classical literature nor the New Testament provides any evidence that the usage extended beyond these limits. Bird's supposed examples in Mark do not belong to any of the three categories mentioned, and there is no justification for his assumption of a general asseverative use.

The second proposition may be dealt with more briefly. No references are given in support of the claim that γάρ is used in an "assertive-allusive" sense when Jesus refers to the Scriptures without explicit quotation, and there are, in fact, no conclusive examples to be found. It is true that some of the γάρ-clauses in the sayings of Jesus reflect the ideas and the vocabulary of the Old Testament, but the particle itself is used in its ordinary explanatory sense. The saying in Mk. x 27, πάντα γάρ δυνατά παρά τῷ θεῷ, is printed as a quotation in Vincent Taylor's text, [3] and in his notes he gives references to Gen. xviii 14; Job x 13; xlii 2; Zech. viii 6. [4]

---

[1] See Denn., p. 64.
[2] See Denn., p. 60.
[3] *The Gospel according to St Mark*, p. 432.
[4] Gen. xviii 14: μὴ ἀδυνατεῖ παρὰ τῷ θεῷ ῥῆμα; Job x 13: ταῦτα ἔχων ἐν σεαυτῷ οἶδα ὅτι πάντα δύνασαι, ἀδυνατεῖ δέ σοι οὐθέν. xlii 2: οἶδα ὅτι πάντα δύνασαι, ἀδυνατεῖ δέ σοι οὐθέν. Zech. viii 6: διότι εἰ ἀδυνατήσει ἐνώπιον τῶν καταλοίπων τοῦ λαοῦ τούτου . . . μὴ καὶ ἐνώπιον ἐμοῦ ἀδυνατήσει;

But the existence here of an allusion to the Old Testament must be deduced from the contents of the clause as a whole. The particle γάρ simply shows that the following clause is intended as an explanation of the preceding statement: παρὰ ἀνθρώποις ἀδύνατον, ἀλλ' οὐ παρὰ θεῷ. In the same way, the γάρ-clauses in the Eschatological Discourse may reflect the apocalyptic ideas of the Old Testament, but in each case the particle itself functions merely as an explanatory connective. [1] Thus there is no reason to suppose that the use of γάρ in recognizable allusions to the Old Testament is anything other than explanatory, or that it has in itself any special exegetical significance.

It would therefore appear that the hypothesis of an affirmatory use of γάρ which is employed in an allusive sense in Mark is an extremely precarious basis for the interpretation of those few Marcan γάρ-clauses in which the normal explanatory force seems at first sight to be unsuitable. In fact, this is half admitted by Bird himself, for, while his main argument proceeds on the lines already indicated, he nevertheless says that he has assumed "that *gar* always remains in some sense expository or explicative." The only remaining means of justifying his theory would be to demonstrate that the γάρ-clauses to which he specifically refers can be explained in no other way. Here, too, his argument is unconvincing.

Two of his examples present no difficulty whatsoever, and may be quoted without further comment. In both cases γάρ is clearly explanatory of the preceding sentence. (a) καὶ λέγει αὐτοῖς, δεῦτε ὑμεῖς αὐτοὶ κατ' ἰδίαν εἰς ἔρημον τόπον, καὶ ἀναπαύσασθε ὀλίγον. ἦσαν γὰρ οἱ ἐρχόμενοι καὶ οἱ ὑπάγοντες πολλοί, καὶ οὐδὲ φαγεῖν εὐκαίρουν (Mk. vi 31). (b) ἀλλ' ὃς ἂν θέλη μέγας γενέσθαι ἐν ὑμῖν, ἔσται ὑμῶν διάκονος, καὶ ὃς ἂν θέλη ἐν ὑμῖν εἶναι πρῶτος, ἔσται πάντων δοῦλος· καὶ γὰρ ὁ υἱὸς τοῦ ἀνθρώπου οὐκ ἦλθεν διακονηθῆναι ἀλλὰ διακονῆσαι . . . . (Mk. x 43-45).

A third instance seems due to a misreading of the text. Referring to Mk. xi 13, Bird says that it is difficult to suggest a motive for the cursing of the tree when it was not the season of figs. This may be true enough. But the γάρ-clause, ὁ γὰρ καιρὸς οὐκ ἦν σύκων, is not

---

[1] E.g. Mk. xiii 19: ἔσονται γὰρ αἱ ἡμέραι ἐκεῖναι θλῖψις οἵα οὐ γέγονεν τοιαύτη ἀπ' ἀρχῆς κτίσεως, cf. Dan. xii 1: ἐκείνη ἡ ἡμέρα θλίψεως οἵα οὐκ ἐγενήθη ἀφ' οὗ ἐγενήθησαν ἕως τῆς ἡμέρας ἐκείνης (see Taylor, *op. cit.*, p. 514). The Marcan γάρ, however, is used simply because the phrase which it introduces explains the preceding "woe" and the advice to pray that the θλῖψις may not happen in winter.

intended as an explanation of the cursing but of the fact that the tree bore no fruit. In itself, the γάρ is perfectly intelligible.

The other occurrences, which require more detailed consideration, are Mk. i 16; ii 15; v 42; xvi 8. For these examples, also, it is possible to find a linguistic explanation which is based upon the ordinary causal function of γάρ.

Writers who use γάρ frequently, as Mark does, are not always logical thinkers who develop an argument stage by stage, representing each further statement as the necessary deduction from the previous one, or who tell a story in strict chronological sequence, with every detail in its logical position in the narrative. In argument, they tend to set down the conclusion first and then to explain in a series of γάρ-clauses the considerations which led up to it. [1] In narrative they mention first the important or striking points in the story, and then fit in the explanatory details afterwards by using γάρ, whether or not these details should logically precede the main points. There is an excellent example of this method of story-telling in Mk. vi 16-18. The chief point is that Herod thought that Jesus was John the Baptist, whom he had executed. The fact of the execution is partially explained in a γάρ-clause which tells the reader that Herod had imprisoned John because of his own marriage with Herodias, and this statement, again, is explained by a further γάρ-clause which indicates that John had denounced the marriage as contrary to the law. The sequence of events is related backwards, as it were, and the fact which in strict logic should have been mentioned at the beginning of the section is left until the end.

This way of thinking and this method of narration produce the phenomena which Bird notices in the γάρ-clauses which he finds tautologous or difficult. They derive from the ordinary explanatory use of γάρ, and parallel instances can be found in Herodotus, whom Denniston mentions as a classical representative of this type of narrative style. [2]

In Mk. ii 15, ἦσαν γὰρ πολλοί, καὶ ἠκολούθουν αὐτῷ, we simply have a further illustration of the fact that Mark tells a story by putting down the main points first. The striking element in this particular story is the fact that Jesus was actually eating a meal with social outcasts. The logically prior information that they had been following him to listen to his teaching is added afterwards, in an

---

[1] See Denn., p. 58, and the example to which he refers in Hdt. III 80.
[2] P. 58.

explanatory γάρ-clause. A similar use of γάρ to introduce an explanatory afterthought is found in Herodotus's description of the customs of the Tauri. They sacrifice to Artemis all the Greeks who are shipwrecked or captured: οἱ μὲν δὴ λέγουσι ὡς τὸ σῶμα ἀπὸ τοῦ κρημνοῦ ὠθέουσι κάτω (ἐπὶ γὰρ κρημνοῦ ἵδρυται τὸ ἱρόν) (Hdt. IV 103).

In another Marcan γάρ-clause, which Bird does not cite, the displacing of explanatory details has developed further: καὶ ἔλεγον πρὸς ἑαυτάς, τίς ἀποκυλίσει ἡμῖν τὸν λίθον ἐκ τῆς θύρας τοῦ μνημείου; καὶ ἀναβλέψασαι θεωροῦσιν ὅτι ἀνακεκύλισται ὁ λίθος· ἦν γὰρ μέγας σφόδρα (Mk. xvi 3-4). The mention of the size of the stone should logically precede the women's question, or at any rate the statement that the stone had been moved. But since, on the one hand, the interest at the beginning of the story is focused upon the actions of the women, and, on the other hand, the really striking point in the narrative is the fact of the stone's removal, these elements are recorded first. Then the Evangelist remembers that he should have mentioned the size of the stone in order to account for the women's anxiety about moving it, and this is added last of all in a γάρ-clause which bears no logical relation to the immediately preceding sentence but which is nevertheless genuinely explanatory.

This way of telling a story may easily result in tautology. Bird complains that in Mk. i 16 ἦσαν γὰρ ἁλιεῖς is a "tautologous and lame explanation" of ἀμφιβάλλοντας ἐν τῇ θαλάσσῃ. But it is only the order in which these separate items of information occur which produces this effect. A more logical narrator might well have written: καὶ παράγων παρὰ τὴν θάλασσαν τῆς Γαλιλαίας εἶδεν ἁλιεῖς τινας, Σίμωνα καὶ Ἀνδρέαν τὸν ἀδελφὸν τοῦ Σίμωνος, ἀμφιβάλλοντας ἐν τῇ θαλάσσῃ. There would be nothing particularly tautologous in mentioning fishermen, their names, and what they were doing at the precise moment when Jesus saw them. In actual fact, the greater narrative interest of the last two items in the series has displaced the first, which appears as a rather unnecessary afterthought. The same tautologous effect is produced by some of the γάρ-clauses in Herodotus, e.g. οὗτος ὁ λέων, ἐπείτε κατεκαίετο ὁ ἐν Δελφοῖσι νηός, κατέπεσε ἀπὸ τῶν ἡμιπλινθίων (ἐπὶ γὰρ τούτοισι ἵδρυτο) καὶ νῦν κεῖται ἐν τῷ Κορινθίων θησαυρῷ (Hdt. I 50). [1] A further example of this style of writing occurs in the Septuagint: ἐγένετο δὲ ἐν τῷ ἀφιέναι αὐτὴν τὴν

---

[1] Cf. I 77; 215.

ψυχήν — ἀπέθνῃσκεν γάρ — ἐκάλεσεν .... (Gen. xxxv 18). Finally, there is in one of the papyri a γάρ-clause which affords an interesting parallel to Mk. i 16: Συρίων γὰρ μετὰ τὸν θάνατον τοῦ πατρὸς τῶν παίδων ἐποφθαλμιάσας τοῖς θρέμμασιν τοῖς ὑπὸ τοῦ πατρὸς αὐτῶν καταλιφθεῖσιν, ποιμὴν γὰρ ἐτύγχανεν, ἐξήκοντα ὄντα τὸν ἀριθμὸν ἥρπασεν .... (P. Thead. 15). [1]

The much-disputed γάρ-clause which concludes Mk. xvi 8 is perhaps analogous both to Mk. i 16 and to xvi 4. According to the earlier manuscripts, the last verse of the Gospel reads: καὶ ἐξελθοῦσαι ἔφυγον ἀπὸ τοῦ μνημείου, εἶχεν γὰρ αὐτὰς τρόμος καὶ ἔκστασις· καὶ οὐδενὶ οὐδὲν εἶπαν, ἐφοβοῦντο γάρ (Mk. xvi 8). It is possible that the final γάρ-clause, as in xvi 4, has been displaced by an item of greater interest, and that it should precede καὶ οὐδενὶ οὐδὲν εἶπαν. This would give an effect of tautology after the mention of τρόμος καὶ ἔκστασις, but, as in i 16, this would be due only to the order in which the various elements in the verse occurred. It would not be tautologous to say, first, that when they heard the message given to them by the young man they were afraid, secondly, that their fear was of the violent sort which produced τρόμος and ἔκστασις, and thirdly, that they rushed precipitately from the tomb. On the other hand, it is perhaps simpler to assume that ἐφοβοῦντο γάρ explains the immediately preceding sentence. In either case there is no difficulty over the function of γάρ, which remains an ordinary explanatory connective.

The last example for discussion is Mk. v 42: καὶ εὐθὺς ἀνέστη τὸ κοράσιον καὶ περιεπάτει· ἦν γὰρ ἐτῶν δώδεκα. Bird rightly claims that if the γάρ-clause is intended as an explanation of the preceding sentence it is an impossible anticlimax. As he points out, Codex Bezae is at a loss to find any causal relation between the two sentences, and replaces γάρ by δέ. Nor is there any element further back in the story to which an explanatory γάρ might be referred (as in xvi 4). Nevertheless, it is possible to account for this occurrence, also, by means of the theory of Mark's use of causal γάρ which has been outlined above. It has been suggested that the Evangelist employs γάρ-clauses to fit in supplementary and explanatory details of his narrative which have been forced from their logical position by more striking elements in the story. If this is so, there may be a further development of the idiom which would be

---

[1] See Hunt and Edgar, *Select Papyri*, No. 262.

somewhat comparable to the classical development of progressive γάρ in questions. Just as the connection of γάρ with questions came to be a stronger factor than its original causal significance, so in the kind of narrative style used by Mark the connection of the particle with supplementary details may have become stronger than the explanatory force which originally caused it to be used to introduce such details, and it may be employed for this purpose where a causal connective is in no way appropriate. At any rate, the style of Herodotus furnishes at least one parallel example of a γάρ-clause which provides an item of supplementary information in no way causally related to the preceding section of the narrative: ἐπεὰν γὰρ ἐς τὴν γῆν ἐκβῇ ἐκ τοῦ ὕδατος ὁ κροκόδειλος καὶ ἔπειτα χάνῃ (ἔωθε γὰρ τοῦτο ὡς ἐπίπαν ποιέειν πρὸς τὸν ζέφυρον), ἐνθαῦτα ὁ τροχίλος ἐσδύνων ἐς τὸ στόμα αὐτοῦ καταπίνει τὰς βδέλλας (Hdt. II 68).

It would therefore appear that there is no reliable linguistic basis for Bird's theory. There is no reason to suppose the existence of a general affirmatory use of γάρ, in Mark or elsewhere, and the supposed difficulties in the Marcan use of γάρ which are held to point to a deeper symbolic meaning can all be resolved by a closer investigation of the type of narrative style in which explanatory γάρ predominates. The parallel examples in Herodotus show that there is nothing unusual about the Marcan occurrences. This being so, there are no grounds for supposing that the use of γάρ is in itself significant from the point of view of the detection of underlying symbolism. Some of Bird's suggestions concerning the Old Testament background of the Gospel may well be plausible, but the existence of symbolism of this kind must be deduced from the material content of the γάρ-clauses and their total context, and not from the fact that γάρ is the introductory particle.

2. Zerwick's theory of the Marcan use of δέ

Zerwick [1] examines in detail the use of καί and δέ as connectives in Mark, and reaches the following conclusions. The natural presupposition for the use of δέ is the existence of a contrast. But contrasts in Mark are not always indicated by δέ, since καί is not infrequently used as a connective where there is a strong and obvious antithesis. What is more, δέ can equally well occur where there is no trace of contradiction at all. The reason for the use of

---

[1] Max Zerwick, *Untersuchungen zum Markus-Stil*, Rome, 1937.

δέ would therefore appear to be psychological rather than logical. It might consist, as in Mk. x, of a stronger feeling for the unity and coherence of some particular dialogue, or of an increased concern on the part of the narrator with the events he is describing, as in the two Trial scenes. Zerwick then gives several more detailed examples of what he means by this "psychological" use of δέ.

It will be necessary to consider these examples individually. There are, however, several general and preliminary observations which can be made. First, Zerwick's theory seems originally to derive from his assumption that δέ is above all an adversative particle, and that it is in place as a connective only where there is at least some hint of a contrast. [1] Where he fails to find this adversative relation he supposes that some non-linguistic factor must be introduced to explain the particle's occurrence. But his conception of the function of δέ is obviously far too much restricted, for there are numerous examples, both classical and Hellenistic, of its use as a purely continuative particle. In illustration of the classical use Denniston [2] refers to the following passage from Plato: ἐπὶ τῇ πυρᾷ κείμενος ἀνεβίω, ἀναβιοὺς δ' ἔλεγεν ἃ ἐκεῖ ἴδοι . . . ἀφικνεῖσθαι σφᾶς εἰς τόπον τινὰ δαιμόνιον, ἐν ᾧ τῆς τε γῆς δύ' εἶναι χάσματα ἐχομένω ἀλλήλοιν καὶ τοῦ οὐρανοῦ αὖ ἐν τῷ ἄνω ἄλλα καταντικρύ. δικαστὰς δὲ μεταξὺ τού-των καθῆσθαι . . . καὶ ἀσπάζεσθαί τε ἀλλήλας . . . διηγεῖσθαι δὲ ἀλλή-λαις . . . . (R. 614 B-E). [3] As an example from Hellenistic literature one can quote a few sentences from Polybius: ὁ δὲ τῶν Καρχηδονίων ναύαρχος . . . ἐτήρει, βουλόμενος διακωλύειν τοὺς ἐπὶ τὸ στρατόπεδον πλέοντας. προσαγγειλάντων δὲ τῶν σκοπῶν πλῆθος ἱκανὸν πλοίων προσφέρεσθαι παντοδαπῶν καὶ συνεγγίζειν, ἀναχθεὶς ἔπλει . . . ὁμοίως δὲ καὶ τοῖς ἐκ τῶν Συρακουσῶν προαπεσταλμένοις ταμίαις ἀνήγγειλαν οἱ προπλεῖν εἰθισμένοι λέμβοι τὸν ἐπίπλουν τῶν ὑπεναντίων (Polyb. I 53, 7-9). [4] From the papyri Mayser [5] quotes a private letter: ἐάν τι δέηι

_____

[1] Op. cit., p. 6.   [2] P. 162.
[3] Cf. R. 359 D — 360 A. The following phrases illustrate continuative δέ: ἰδόντα δὲ καὶ θαυμάσαντα . . . συλλόγου δὲ γενομένου . . . τούτου δὲ γενομέ-νου . . . αἰσθόμενον δὲ εὐθύς . . . ἐλθόντα δὲ καὶ τὴν γυναῖκα αὐτοῦ. See also Xen. Instit. Cyri I ii 7-8 διδάσκουσι δὲ τοὺς παῖδας καὶ σωφροσύνην . . . διδάσ-κουσι δὲ αὐτοὺς καὶ πείθεσθαι τοῖς ἄρχουσι . . . διδάσκουσι δὲ καὶ ἐγκράτειαν γαστρὸς καὶ ποτοῦ (cf. Thuc. I 46-47).
[4] There are also examples in several books of the Septuagint: Esther vi 2, εὗρεν δὲ . . . 3 εἶπεν δὲ ὁ βασιλεύς . . . 4 εἶπεν δὲ ὁ βασιλεύς . . . 6 εἶπεν δὲ ὁ βασιλεύς . . . 7 εἶπεν δὲ πρὸς τὸν βασιλέα . . . 11 ἔλαβεν δὲ Αμαν τὴν στολήν . . . 12 ἐπέστρεψεν δὲ ὁ Μαρδοχαῖος εἰς τὴν αὐλήν. Cf. II Macc. i 20-23, ὡς δὲ διε-σάφησαν ἡμῖν . . . ὡς δὲ ἀνηνέχθη τὰ τῶν θυσιῶν . . . ὡς δὲ ἐγένετο τοῦτο . . . προσευχὴν δὲ ἐποιήσαντο οἱ ἱερεῖς.   [5] P. 126.

ἀναλῶσαι, δός, παρὰ δὲ ἡμῶν κομιεῖ. ἀπόστειλον δὲ ἡμῖν καὶ Ζηνόβιον. ἐχέτω δὲ καὶ ἱματισμὸν ὡς ἀστειότατον. κόμισαι δὲ καὶ τὸν ἔριφον παρὰ Ἀρίστωνος . . . ἀπόστειλον δὲ ἡμῖν καὶ τυροὺς καὶ κέραμον καινὸν καὶ λάχανα. ἐμβαλοῦ δὲ αὐτὰ καὶ φυλακίτας, οἳ συνδιακομιοῦσιν τὸ πλοῖον (P. Hib. 54). The use of δέ as a continuative particle in Mark is in no way surprising, and would hardly seem to call for a special explanation.

Secondly, Zerwick fails to take into consideration the fact that the use of the definite article as a demonstrative pronoun *ipso facto* necessitates its combination with δέ and therefore the use of δέ rather than καί as the connective. Mark is particularly fond of this idiom, [1] and uses it some 38 times. In the following instances the force of δέ is clearly adversative, and so of no importance in connection with the present argument: i 45; iii 4; vii 6; viii 33; ix 32, 34; x 3, 22, 48; xii 15; xiv 20, 31, 52, 61, 68, 70, 71; xv 14 b. But there are several occasions when δέ appears to be continuative, and there ὁ δέ would mean "and he" rather than "but he." This occurs in the following passages: v 34; vi 24, 49; viii 5, 28; ix 21; x 4, (20), 26, 36, 39, 50; xi 6; xii 16 (*bis*); xiv (11), 46; xv 13. Several of these references are found in passages which are especially mentioned by Zerwick as examples of the "psychological" use of δέ: v 34; vi 24; viii 5; x 50; xii 16; xv 13. He refers also to vii 28, but here it is not clear whether ἡ δέ is continuative or adversative. Vincent Taylor maintains that "the word of Jesus is not rejected, but carried a stage farther." [2] But if Ναί is omitted, [3] it would be possible to interpret the reply as a protest, and so to attach an adversative force to δέ. [4] Now Zerwick may well be correct in detecting an effect of emphasis in the verses to which he refers. But if so, this will not be due to an unusual use of δέ to indicate progression rather than opposition. The emphatic effect

---

[1] It is found in classical literature, e.g. Xen. *Inst. Cyri* I iii 13: ἡ δὲ ἀπεκρίνατο . . . iii 15: ὁ δὲ οὐκ ἐμέλλησεν . . . iv 7: οἱ δ᾽ ἔλεγον . . . According to Mayser, it is used frequently in the papyri (p. 128). As an example he quotes: Ἀρτεμίδωρον ἀπῃτοῦμεν· ὁ δ᾽ οὐκ ἔφη πρὸς αὐτὸν εἶναι (Zen. P. 59150, 16).

[2] *Op. cit.* p. 351.

[3] See C. H. Turner, "Marcan Usage: Notes, Critical and Exegetical, on the Second Gospel, VII," *Journal of Theological Studies*, xxviii (1926), 19-20.

[4] A similar difficulty of interpretation arises in ix 12. Taylor thinks that the verse indicates that Jesus agrees with the disciples that Elijah must come first, but he also quotes the view of Wellhausen, who would take the whole verse as a question which rejects this idea (*op. cit.*, p. 394).

will be due simply to the use of a demonstrative pronoun. And since, in Mark, the use of a demonstrative as the subject of the sentence means in four out of every five cases the use of the definite article combined with δέ, [1] the use of δέ as a connective in these instances is a grammatical necessity, and needs no further explanation.

Thirdly, some comments are necessary on the distinction drawn by Zerwick between the dialogues in the earlier chapters of the Gospel and those in chapter x. He maintains that in chapter x the dialogue has its own inherent significance, whereas in the first five chapters its function is merely to act as an introduction either to a notable saying of Jesus or to one of his miracles. [2] In chapter x the particle δέ predominates. Since it is a particle which looks backward and indicates the connection with what precedes, [3] it shows here the inner coherence of the dialogue (indicating, presumably, that each separate element is of equivalent importance). In chapters i-v, where it is unnecessary to do this, καί predominates as the connective. The function of δέ in chapter x is classed by Zerwick as a "psychological" use.

Now it may readily be admitted that his general distinction between the contents of chapter x and those of chapters i-v is a valid one, and also that the comparative neglect of δέ in these earlier chapters and its predominance in chapter x are not wholly arbitrary phenomena, but are due, as he suggests, to the fact that in chapter x the author is interested in the dialogue as such, whereas in chapters i-v he does not regard it as dialogue proper but as so much narrative introduction. But the conclusion by no means follows that we have in chapter x some different use of δέ which is to be termed "psychological." The reason for its presence is simply that it is the obvious particle to use in dialogue for the purpose of introducing the different speakers, and this, again, is because of its double function as a continuative and as an adversative connective. If the speakers advance opposing points of view, its suitability needs no further justification. On the other hand, the relation between the contribution of one speaker and that of the

---

[1] αὐτός occurs as follows: i 8; iv 27; iv 38; v 40; viii 29; xiv 15; xiv 44; (7 times). αὐτή is found at x 12. ἐκεῖνος is used pronominally only in iv 20 and vii 20. οὗτος is used pronominally as the subject only in direct speech.

[2] *Op. cit.*, p. 9.

[3] *Ibid.*, p. 6.

next may be purely progressive, with no trace of contradiction. Here a continuative particle would primarily be required. And yet the fact that two speakers are involved does introduce a slight feeling of contrast. Both nuances are adequately expressed by δέ in virtue of its double function. But this function is the ordinary, logical, grammatical one which it normally performs. Further, the impression of inner coherence in the dialogues in chapter x is due to a considerable extent to the use of ὁ δέ as a demonstrative pronoun which, by providing a backward reference to some person in the preceding sentence, serves to throw the attention of the reader back to the previous statement. But the use of δέ in this idiom, as has been mentioned already, is conditioned wholly by the grammatical factor. And in so far as the general effect of contrast between the various speakers serves to give coherence to the dialogue as a whole, this, too, derives from the normal function of δέ.

These preliminary observations suggest that there are grounds for doubting the validity of Zerwick's interpretation of δέ in Mark. A just estimation can be arrived at, however, only after examining in detail the individual examples which he brings forward in support of the theory that the use of δέ is of psychological rather than linguistic significance. [1] It is necessary to point out here that in several of the verses to which he refers the occurrence of δέ is textually doubtful, and may be the result of the substitution of δέ for an original καί. The verses in question are these: vi 22, 37, 38; xiv 64; xv 2, 15. The number of variants, however, is not in itself sufficient to invalidate Zerwick's theory as a whole, and it is not necessary, on the other hand, to disprove the existence of δέ in the passages in order to disprove the general hypothesis. It has therefore seemed simpler, for the purposes of the present argument, to accept the reading δέ where it is accepted by Zerwick himself, since there is also in most cases a fairly substantial degree of manuscript evidence in its favor.

(a) Mk. xiv 66-71

This section is concerned with Peter's denial. Zerwick maintains that the regular alternation of καί and δέ as connectives and the fact that δέ is used only to introduce each of the three denials produce a rhythm of thought which serves the purpose of keeping

---

[1] *Op. cit.*, pp. 15 ff.

before the reader's mind the conception of the triple denial as a single whole. If no such psychological significance attaches to the use of δέ, why is it not employed in verse 69, where, in the altercation between Peter and the maidservant, Peter's attempt to escape is countered by her observation of it and the repetition of her previous remark?

The alternation of connectives, however, is by no means as regular as Zerwick implies. He reproduces the sequence as follows: καί . . . δέ . . . καί . . . δέ . . . καί . . . δέ . . . . But in doing so he has omitted some of the connectives altogether, and he also omits verse 72. This should surely be included in any consideration of the pericope as a whole, since it constitutes an integral part of it. The following scheme is a more accurate reproduction of the pattern of connecting particles: καί (maid subject) . . . καί (maid subj.) . . . ὁ δέ (Peter subj.) . . . καί (Peter subj.) . . . καί (maid subj.) . . . ὁ δέ (Peter subj.) . . . καί (bystanders subj.) . . . ὁ δέ (Peter subj.) . . . καί (ἀλέκτωρ subj.) . . . καί (Peter subj.) . . . καί (Peter subj.). The pattern is irregular, and Zerwick's hypothetical rhythm is difficult to discover. Further, while it is obviously true that Peter's denials are the point of interest and emphasis, and also that these are introduced by δέ, both the indication of emphasis and also the occurrence of δέ are the result of the use of ὁ δέ as a demonstrative pronoun, which refers, in its customary fashion, to a person who has already been mentioned in an oblique case. [1] Here we have ἐμβλέψασα αὐτῷ λέγει . . . ὁ δέ . . . ἰδοῦσα αὐτὸν ἤρξατο πάλιν λέγειν . . . ὁ δέ . . . οἱ παρεστῶτες ἔλεγον τῷ Πέτρῳ . . . ὁ δέ . . . . Where there is already a perfectly normal linguistic explanation for the use of δέ, it seems unnecessary to search for any more obscure meaning in its occurrence. And the failure to use δέ in verse 69 where Zerwick sees an adversative connection of thought may be accounted for by supposing that the Evangelist himself was more conscious of the continuative connection which derives from the repetition of the maidservant's previous assertion.

(b) xiv 26-31

Zerwick suggests that here the Evangelist has in mind Peter's forthcoming denial, and that it is therefore Peter who is introduced by the particle δέ. But it is doubtful whether Mark intends that the

---

[1] See Robertson, *A Grammar of the Greek New Testament*, p. 695.

attention of his readers should be focused entirely upon Peter. The fulfilment of an Old Testament prophecy (verse 27) is of interest in itself; verse 28, which has no specific reference to Peter as an individual, is taken up again in the final chapter (xvi 7), and may be of particular significance if "Galilee," as has been suggested, [1] is a reference to the Gentile mission. It is not particularly clear whether Zerwick is arguing here that the Evangelist is especially interested in Peter and that this proves that the use of δέ has a psychological significance, or whether he is maintaining that the use of δέ here can only be attributed to a psychological factor and that it therefore shows that Mark is especially interested in Peter. If the first alternative is correct, the attribution of significance to other elements in the pericope will weaken the argument for the psychological significance of δέ. If the second is correct, it must be pointed out that δέ in verses 29 and 31 is perfectly comprehensible without resorting to a psychological explanation. The first is adversative, introducing Peter's contradiction of Christ's prophecy, the second forms part of the demonstrative pronoun, and is also adversative.

(c) vi 35-38

Here the whole interest of the Evangelist is said to be concentrated upon Christ's replies to the bewildered disciples, with the result that the replies are introduced by δέ. What emphasis there is, however, derives from the use of the demonstrative pronoun, which also accounts for the use of δέ as the connective.

(d) xiv 60-64, xv 1-15

It is suggested that the two Trial scenes offer examples of the use of δέ to provide an accentuated emotional effect and to indicate the interest of the author at the climax of the narrative. In these two scenes especially, the use of δέ produces a strong feeling of tension, a quickening of the tempo, which plainly conveys the concern of the writer and his lively visualization of the events which he is describing. The scenes rush to a crisis, and each step is of decisive significance. The interpretation of δέ in Mark as an indication of the especial interest of the narrator accords with its exceptionally frequent use in these two sections.

---

[1] See C. F. Evans, " 'I will go before you into Galilee,' " *Journal of Theological Studies*, n.s. v (1954), 3-18.

Now it is perfectly true that the scenes in question do produce an effect of tension and crisis, but this is surely due much more to their subject matter than to the use of any particular connective. In so far as the use of δέ may contribute to the impression one gets that each stage of the proceedings is of vital importance and that the narrator is clearly visualizing the subject of his description, it does so by virtue of its contrasting function, which serves to focus the reader's attention upon each of the opposing parties in turn. But in the second scene this effect is also induced by the fact that in all but one instance (xv 2) each individual character is mentioned specifically by name: ὁ δὲ Πιλᾶτος occurs 6 times within 15 verses. Thus, while Zerwick's appreciation of the psychological effect of the Trial scenes may well be correct, the use of δέ, in proportion to the other elements in the narrative, would appear to contribute rather less to it than he supposes, and its contribution, in any case, derives from the normal grammatical function of the particle. In support of his theory he alleges that δέ is exceptionally frequent in these sections, so that its use must be attributed to some factor other than the purely linguistic one. But in the first scene δέ is no more frequent than in a pericope of similar length in chapter x; in xiv 60-64 δέ occurs 4 times to introduce the different speakers, while in x 35-40 it occurs 5 times with the same function. The second scene is considerably longer, and δέ is proportionately more frequent. The only conclusion the evidence warrants is that δέ is a frequent, and obviously suitable, particle to use in reported dialogue.

Zerwick concludes his consideration of the Trial scenes by remarking that some of the tension which they exhibit is to be seen also in the story about tribute to Caesar (xii 13-17), where δέ occurs 4 times as a connective. In three of these occurrences, however, it is part of the demonstrative and needs no further explanation.

(e) vii 28

Zerwick believes that δέ is used here because the Evangelist thinks of the following saying as the climax of the story. Again, however, it is part of the demonstrative pronoun, so that, if the emphasis does lie here, [1] this is probably due to the use of the demonstrative as such, and not specifically to the use of δέ.

---

[1] Cf. Joachim Jeremias, *Jesus' Promise to the Nations* (*Studies in Biblical Theology*, No. 24), London, 1958, p. 30.

(f) vi 17-29

Zerwick maintains that δέ stands here at the critical points in the narrative: at verse 19, the first mention of the enmity of Herodias towards John the Baptist; at verse 22, where the king rashly invites her daughter to ask for whatever she wants; and at verse 24, where the daughter is instructed by her mother to ask for the Baptist's head. Simply from the linguistic point of view one would expect δέ to be used also at verse 24, to introduce the girl's reaction to the king's promise, at verse 26, to indicate his reaction to the unexpected request, and at verse 27, to mark the carrying out of the order for John's execution.

This argument from the absence of δέ where, linguistically, one might have expected it to occur is singularly unconvincing. Zerwick offers no explanation of why he considers δέ more suitable than καί in verse 24; in verse 26 it is not the king's unfavorable reaction to the request which is the significant point, but the fact that, although he regrets doing so, he nevertheless complies with the girl's demand, so that a continuative particle is perfectly suitable; nor does there seem to be any reason why the carrying out of an order should be introduced by δέ rather than καί. [1] If this criticism is valid, the only real justification for attaching a non-linguistic significance to δέ in the rest of the narrative would be the impossibility of explaining its occurrence in linguistic terms. The examples Zerwick points to, however, are linguistically easily explicable. The last of the three (verse 24) forms part of the demonstrative pronoun, the use of which here, referring back to τῇ μητρὶ αὐτῆς, is entirely natural. The second (verse 22) may be simply continuative. It has been remarked already [2] that the continuative use of δέ is common in both classical and Hellenistic Greek. This verse apart, it occurs in Mark as follows: i 32; v 33; ix 25; x 21, 24, 39, 51; xii 17, 26; xiii 5, 7, 17; xiv 9, 31, 62, 63; xv 4, 9, 15. There is therefore no reason to doubt that this is the explanation of δέ in vi 22. The first example (verse 19) is probably to be understood as inceptive. It is at verse 19 that the author appears to realize that if he intends to tell in detail the story of John's death it will be

---

[1] To take a random example, in the book of Esther there are ten occasions when the carrying out of an order is described. Of these, seven are introduced by καί: i 15; iv 12; iv 17; v 14; vii 10; viii 9; ix 14; three are introduced by δέ: iv 9; vi 2; vi 11.

[2] See above, pp. 51-52.

impossible to continue narrating the events backwards by means of γάρ-clauses, and so he starts again, with the announcement of the enmity of Herodias, who is the real agent of the execution and who sets in train the events immediately leading up to it. There are several other occurrences of inceptive δέ in Mark. Three occur in narrative: i 30; xv 6, 16; four in discourse: iv 15; xiii 9, 14, 28. This inceptive use is attested in both classical and Hellenistic literature. In the first book of Thucydides, after the introduction to the account of the Peloponnesian War, the narrative proper begins: τῶν δὲ πρότερον ἔργων μέγιστον ἐπράχθη τὸ Μηδικόν... (Thuc. I 23). [1] In Plutarch's life of Theseus there is a section in which each separate exploit of the hero is introduced by inceptive δέ, [2] and for examples from the Septuagint we may refer to several instances in Esther. [3]

(g) x 46-52

The interest of the Evangelist is said to be concentrated upon the behavior of Bartimaeus, who is always introduced by δέ. This is especially significant in verse 50, since the carrying out of a command in Mark is normally introduced by καί. (This statement completely contradicts Zerwick's earlier assertion that one would have expected δέ to be used at vi 27 to mark the carrying out of the king's order.) Moreover, the fact that Bartimaeus is expressly mentioned by name also shows that the Evangelist is especially interested in him. This is no doubt true, but is hardly an argument for a special use of δέ. In two out of the three occurrences it is attached to demonstrative ὁ (verses 48 and 50); the third (verse 51) is continuative. Further, if Zerwick's theory were correct, one would expect to find δέ used at the beginning of verse 47 also (καὶ ἀκούσας ... ἤρξατο κράζειν).

(h) v 25-34

The interest of the Evangelist both in the woman herself and also in Jesus' answer to her is shown by the use of δέ in verses 33 and 34. But these occurrences are in themselves entirely normal. The second is part of the demonstrative pronoun; the first introduces the second chief participant in the dialogue.

---

[1] Cf. I 11 αἴτιον δ' ἦν οὐχ ἡ ὀλιγανθρωπία τοσοῦτον ὅσον ἡ ἀχρηματία...
I 13 δυνατωτέρας δὲ γιγνομένης τῆς Ἑλλάδος....

[2] *Vit. Par.* I i Thes. viii ff.

[3] E.g. vi 1 ὁ δὲ κύριος ...; ix 20 ἔγραψεν δὲ ...; x 1 ἔγραψεν δὲ ὁ βασιλεὺς ....

(i) v 35-43

Much the same interpretation is offered of the use of δέ in the account of the healing of Jairus's daughter. The change of subject, in so far as it concerns Jesus, is marked by δέ at least as far as the climax of the story. But this exception surely goes a long way towards invalidating the theory which Zerwick proposes. Are we to suppose that the interest of the Evangelist in his story suddenly waned at the precise point when the healing—a remarkable one— took place: καὶ εὐθὺς ἀνέστη τὸ κοράσιον καὶ περιεπάτει? In any case, as Zerwick himself admits, the two occurrences of δέ (verses 36 and 40) are explicable as simply adversative.

(j) xii 7

Zerwick points out that δέ stands here at the climax of the narrative. That is true, but it is also the natural and logical particle to use in this context. Zerwick argues that if δέ were employed by Mark in accordance with its normal and logical force we should find it also in the preceding verses which describe the reaction of the tenants to the slaves who were first sent to them. But from the point of view of the narrator and the readers the treatment of the slaves might be regarded as the expected and inevitable thing to happen, in which case an adversative particle would not be required.

(k) viii 1-10

Zerwick discounts the theory that this is a doublet of the miracle in chapter vi, and maintains that the most natural explanation is that Mark knew of two miraculous feedings in which the numbers of the people concerned were different. The distinction is not of real importance, but for the purpose of remembering the stories as separate ones during the oral period of transmission the difference in numbers would instinctively be emphasized. And the only use of δέ in this section occurs in the sentences in which we are told that there were seven loaves and four thousand people. From the stylistic viewpoint one could use δέ as a connective in verses 4, 5, 6c, 7a, but it does not in fact occur here, although it does occur in some of the parallel verses in chapter vi. The only objection to the theory that δέ is employed here to emphasize the difference in numbers is that it is not found in the verse which mentions the seven baskets of fragments. But Mark's grammatical thinking is not of a reflective but of an instinctive nature. He uses δέ to indicate interest or emphasis only at places where it can already stand in its own right. In verse 8, where the subject remains the same throughout, δέ would not be possible without straining the normal usage.

These last remarks surely undermine the whole theory. For, if Mark uses δέ only where it is in any case logically appropriate, what is the problem, and why is any "psychological" explanation necessary? And it seems highly unlikely that an "instinctive" form of grammatical thinking would produce the selective use and avoidance of δέ which Zerwick's hypothesis demands. Both the occurrence and the absence of the particle in this section are explicable in strictly linguistic terms. In the first example (verse 5) it is part of the demonstrative pronoun. In the second (verse 9), it occurs with the imperfect of εἶναι in an explanatory parenthesis describing the circumstances in which the miracle was performed. This is a characteristic Marcan idiom. He frequently uses parenthetical δὲ, preceded by ἦν or ἦσαν, to describe what might be termed the accompanying circumstances of his narrative which, while not themselves constituting a further step in the progress of the story, nevertheless serve to explain the ensuing action. Halfway through the story of the Gadarene demoniac we are told: ἦν δὲ ἐκεῖ . . . ἀγέλη χοίρων μεγάλη βοσκομένη (Mk. v 11). Vincent Taylor [1] maintains that a new stage in the narrative begins here, but it seems better to take the phrase as a parenthesis. It occurs as an insertion in what appears to be a single continuous speech by the demons: καὶ παρεκάλει αὐτὸν πολλὰ ἵνα μὴ αὐτὰ ἀποστείλη ἔξω τῆς χώρας. ἦν δὲ ἐκεῖ . . . . καὶ παρεκάλεσαν αὐτὸν λέγοντες· πέμψον ἡμᾶς εἰς τοὺς χοίρους (Mk. v 10-12). The presence of the herd of swine is not in itself a fresh incident, but it explains the rest of the story. The same is true of xv 7: ἦν δὲ ὁ λεγόμενος Βαραββᾶς μετὰ τῶν στασιαστῶν δεδεμένος. The fact of the imprisonment of Barabbas is not a new event, but the necessary explanation of the following scene between Pilate and the crowd. Two further phrases of this kind (ii 6; xiv 4) describe the attitude of the onlookers during some action of Jesus or an action in which he is concerned, and explain the saying which follows. Others indicate the temporal or local setting of the events narrated, e.g. ἦν δὲ ὥρα τρίτη καὶ ἐσταύρωσαν αὐτόν (Mk. xv 25; cf. xiv 1; x 32). The last example is found in xv

---

[1] *Op. cit.*, p. 282.

40, and other slightly different uses of parenthetical δέ are found at vii 26; xiv 44; xv 47. The use of parenthetical δέ with the imperfect of εἶναι is a fairly widespread idiom, and it is of interest to note that it often occurs in numerical descriptions, as in viii 9. We may quote the following examples: ἔπλεον ἐπὶ τὴν Κέρκυραν ναυσὶ πεντήκοντα καὶ ἑκατόν. ἦσαν δὲ Ἠλείων μὲν δέκα, Μεγαρέων δὲ δώδεκα (Thuc. I 46); ἰσχυρῶς γὰρ ἐδεδοίκει τοὺς Παλλαντίδας ἐπιβουλεύοντας αὐτῷ καὶ διὰ τὴν ἀπαιδίαν καταφρονοῦντας· ἦσαν δὲ πεντήκοντα παῖδες ἐκ Πάλλαντος γεγονότες (Plut. Vit. Par. I i Thes. iii 7); κἀκεῖνος θαρρῶν ἤδη τοῖς ᾠκειωμένοις, ἦσαν δ᾽ εἰς τετρακισμυρίους οἱ Ταριχαιᾶται, παντὶ τῷ πλήθει παρρησιαστικώτερον ὡμίλει (Joseph. de Bell. Jud. II 608); [1] and ὅσα ποτὲ ὑπῆρχεν ἐν ταμιείωι — ἦν δ᾽ ὀλίγα — ἐγὼ αὐτὰ ἐφύτευσα (PSI IV 433, 7). [2] It would therefore appear that the second occurrence of δέ in Mk. viii 1-10, no less than the first, is easily explicable from the linguistic point of view.

Zerwick also argues that δέ is absent where linguistically one would expect its presence, and adduces in support of this assertion the parallel account in chapter vi where the particle does occur. But the differences between the two accounts in this respect, if textually valid, would seem to be due rather to the slightly different way in which the narratives are constructed than to the fact that in chapter viii the particle δέ is reserved for some special use. Most of the verses in viii 1-10 where Zerwick suggests that δέ would have been a suitable connective have no strict parallel in the preceding chapter. The only verse in which the comparison would be precisely applicable is viii 5 (καὶ ἠρώτα αὐτούς, πόσους ἔχετε ἄρτους;), to be contrasted with vi 38 (ὁ δὲ λέγει αὐτοῖς, πόσους ἔχετε ἄρτους;), and here the presence of δέ in chapter vi, if it is the correct reading, and its absence in chapter viii may be due to the fact that, whereas in both accounts it is Jesus who asks the question about the loaves, in the first dialogue, formally speaking, the disciples take the initiative and Jesus responds, but in the second one Jesus himself takes the initiative and the disciples respond. The two conversations can be represented in skeleton form as follows:

vi 35 ff.	viii 1 ff.
καὶ . . . προσελθόντες αὐτῷ οἱ μαθηταὶ αὐτοῦ ἔλεγον ὅτι	προσκαλεσάμενος τοὺς μαθητὰς λέγει αὐτοῖς . . . .

[1] Cf. Philo, de Virt. vii.
[2] See Mayser, p. 188.

ὁ δὲ ἀποκριθεὶς εἶπεν αὐτοῖς . . . .   καὶ ἀπεκρίθησαν αὐτῷ οἱ μαθηταὶ
                                        αὐτοῦ . . . .
καὶ λέγουσιν αὐτῷ . . . .   καὶ ἠρώτα αὐτούς . . . .
ὁ δὲ λέγει αὐτοῖς . . . .   οἱ δὲ εἶπαν . . . .
καὶ . . . λέγουσιν . . . .

On the assumption that the two occurrences of ὁ δέ in vi are textually correct, the formal construction is almost identical. The initiators of the dialogues are further introduced by καί, and it is not thought necessary to specify the subjects of the verbs which relate to them. The subjects of the other half of the conversation, on the other hand, are clearly indicated either by the use of the demonstrative pronoun or by the repetition of the substantive. These facts explain the occurrence of δέ in vi 38 and the use of καί in viii 5; i.e. the construction of the dialogue in chapter vi demands the use of the demonstrative, which, in turn, requires δέ as the connective; whereas the same type of construction in chapter viii leads quite naturally and logically to the use of καί in verse 5, since in this instance the subject of the verb is the initiator of the whole conversation.

The result of this discussion would appear to be that Zerwick fails to substantiate his theory. The uses of δέ which he points to as "psychological" are all capable of a linguistic explanation. The argument that if the Marcan use of δέ were conditioned by strictly grammatical factors it would occur on occasions where καί is found instead is unconvincing, as none of these examples absolutely demands δέ rather than καί, and καί is in any case Mark's favorite connective.

3. Δέ *marking a turning-point in the narrative*

C. H. Turner argues that when Mark uses δέ at the beginning of a paragraph this is an indication that a significant turning-point in the narrative has been reached. [1] He gives the following examples:

  i 14 the beginning of the public ministry of Jesus;
  vii 24 Jesus moves for the first time into Gentile territory;
  x 32 the beginning of the journey to Jerusalem;
  xiv 1 the beginning of the Passion Narrative.

---

[1] "A Textual Commentary on Mark i," *Journal of Theological Studies*, xxviii (1927), 152.

There are, however, certain objections to this theory, both on linguistic and on textual grounds.

The linguistic objections may be mentioned fairly briefly. To substantiate Turner's hypothesis it would seem necessary to be able to maintain the truth of two propositions: first, that the use of δέ in the examples which he quotes can be classified grammatically as inceptive; secondly, that Mark uses inceptive δέ only after a major division between the various sections of his narrative.

The truth of the first proposition is doubtful in respect of two of the examples. In x 32 and xiv 1 we have instances of an idiom which elsewhere in the Gospel is employed to indicate some kind of a parenthesis, i.e. the use of δέ with the imperfect of εἶναι, as ἦσαν δὲ ἐν τῇ ὁδῷ x 32; ἦν δὲ τὸ πάσχα xiv 1. [1] It has been maintained that these parenthetical δέ-clauses beginning with ἦν or ἦσαν, are used by Mark to describe the accompanying circumstances of his narrative rather than the main events, and this interpretation would suit the clauses under discussion quite well, the one describing the local, the other the temporal setting of the following events. In any case, even if an inceptive force be allowed to δέ in these particular clauses, it seems a little unlikely that an idiom which elsewhere is definitely parenthetical should be used, consciously or unconsciously, to indicate that a decisive stage has been reached in the progress of the narrative.

The second proposition is not true at all, for the other Marcan examples of inceptive δέ give no support to it whatsoever. The first, in i 30, ἡ δὲ πενθερὰ Σίμωνος ... simply introduces one of a string of incidents occurring, according to the Evangelist, on the same Sabbath day; vi 19, ἡ δὲ Ἡρῳδιὰς ἐνεῖχεν αὐτῷ begins a story which is in itself a parenthesis from the point of view of the narrative as a whole; and both xv 6, κατὰ δὲ ἑορτὴν ἀπέλυεν αὐτοῖς ἕνα δέσμιον, and xv 16, οἱ δὲ στρατιῶται ἀπήγαγον αὐτόν, begin separate incidents in the Passion Narrative, but hardly constitute major turning-points in the whole Gospel.

The textual objections arise from the fact that in i 14 and also in vii 24 some witnesses read καί instead of δέ. The variants need careful consideration. Before dealing with each one separately it will be useful to mention several general characteristics displayed by the Marcan textual tradition in respect of the occurrences of καί and δέ.

---

[1] See above, pp. 61-62.

First, there appears to have been an overwhelming tendency
for scribes to alter καί to δέ. The evidence in S. C. E. Legg's edition
of Mark shows that there are 87 instances of this process. [1] In some
cases it is the result of assimilation to the text of Matthew, in
others the result of an attempt to clarify the sense by substituting
the demonstrative ὁ δέ for καί followed by a verb with an ambiguous
subject. But in the majority of examples it is simply an attempt at
stylistic improvement.

Secondly, there are very few examples of the reverse process, the
substitution of καί for δέ. If the reading in any given instance could
be settled simply by accepting as correct that given by the substantial majority of witnesses, there would be five or six variants
where it might be maintained with a certain degree of plausibility
that several witnesses had replaced an original δέ by καί. There is,
however, some reason to believe that καί may be the correct
reading even if it is attested by a few manuscripts only. Matthew's
treatment of Mark shows that there was a tendency already
operating in the first century to diminish the instances of καί in
favor of δέ, and both the literary κοινή and also the Atticism of the
second century would favor the substitution of δέ for καί.

Thirdly, in so far as it is possible to generalize about the tendencies
of particular groups of witnesses, it is perhaps worth remarking
that the Alexandrian witnesses are the more reliable in this respect,
and that the Caesarean group, on the other hand, show a very
pronounced tendency to change καί to δέ.

We now come to consider the variants at i 14 and vii 24.

i 14 καὶ μετά   BD *a ff* Sy.[s.] Cop.[boh.] Geo.[2], *item* et factum est post-
                quam *c* vg. (1 MS.)

μετὰ δέ   Uncs. rell. Minusc. omn. Sy.[pesh. hl.] Cop.[sah. boh. (ed.)]
                Geo.[1] Aeth. Arm. Euseb. Aug., *item* postquam autem
                f g² r^2 *vg.* (pler. *et* WW), sed postquam *b d g¹ r¹ t*,
                postquam *tant. l* vg. (1 MS.)

In favor of δέ we have the witness of ℵ and most of the other
Alexandrians. But impressive evidence in favor of καί is provided
by B, with some support from other witnesses. Further, while there
would appear to be no special reason for the substitution of καί for
δέ, it is easy to find reasons for the substitution of δέ for καί. There
is the possibility of assimilation to Mt. iv 12, or the desire for a

---

[1] This total includes all the variants except the two under consideration
here.

change of connective after the preceding καί-sentences; it might be felt necessary to mark the contrast between Jesus' retirement in the desert and the beginning of his public ministry, or to indicate the beginning of the narrative proper by using inceptive δέ. If the general tendency of the scribes to alter καί to δέ is also taken into account, it would seem that καί is for several reasons the reading to be preferred.

vii 24 (a) ἐκεῖθεν (ἐκεῖθε B*) δὲ ἀναστάς

ℵ B L Δ 517 892 Sy.hl. mg.

    (b) κἀκεῖθεν δὲ ἀναστάς   33 579 Cop.boh.

    (c) καὶ ἐκεῖθεν (κἀκεῖθεν 482) ἀναστάς

A N X Γ Θ Π Σ Φ Ϙ fam.1
22 fam.13 543 28 157 565
700 1071 al. pler. *l r*2 *vg.*
Sy.hl. *txt.* Geo.2 Arm.

    (d) καὶ ἀναστὰς ἐκεῖθεν

D *f ff* g1 (= iesus) *q r*1 Geo.1
Aeth.

    (e) καὶ ἀναστάς (om. ἐκεῖθεν)   W *a b i n* Sy.s

The second of these readings is obviously a conflation. The last three, for the purpose of the present discussion, can be regarded as a single group. The evidence here is somewhat difficult to assess. The witness of both ℵ and B in favor of δέ is certainly impressive. On the other hand, the witness of the Caesarean group to καί is very strong evidence in its support, in view of the marked preference for δέ which these manuscripts normally exhibit. Moreover, the preference for δέ is a noticeable individual characteristic of W, which likewise here supports καί. The possibility that καί is correct is perhaps strengthened by the fact that on the three other occasions when Mark uses a similar phrase with ἐκεῖθεν the connecting particle is καί without a textual variant, i.e. καὶ ἐξῆλθεν ἐκεῖθεν vi 1; κἀκεῖθεν ἐξελθόντες, ix 30; καὶ ἐκεῖθεν ἀναστάς x 1.

Thus, the first two examples given by Turner in illustration of his theory are textually doubtful. In i 14 there are fairly strong reasons for preferring the reading καὶ μετά, and there is also good evidence in favor of καί at vii 24. In his remaining examples δέ may be parenthetical rather than inceptive, and it is in any case doubtful whether the other instances of inceptive δέ in Mark would support his theory.

The results of this first section of the inquiry are clearly of a somewhat negative character. They merely show that the attempts to attach to the Marcan particles some further, non-linguistic, significance are on the whole unconvincing. However, since the problem of the construction of Mark is not yet finally resolved, it may be useful to point out that it would be unwise to base either the typological or the chronological approach upon the occurrence of two of the commonest particles in the Greek language. It is not here that the exegetical interest of the particles is to be found, but rather in the various possibilities of interpretation which individual occurrences present in particular verses.

B. INDIVIDUAL PROBLEMS

The interpretation of several verses in the Gospels depends to some extent upon the significance which is to be attached to the particle πλήν. In both the Lucan and the Matthean versions of the prayer of Jesus in Gethsemane πλήν is found where the Marcan version has ἀλλά, and it is of interest to consider whether the change of particle points to a difference of interpretation. There is also some dispute as to the meaning of πλήν in the Matthean version of Jesus' reply to the question of the High Priest at his trial. Two further questions which will arise for discussion in this section are concerned with problems of exegesis in the Corinthian Epistles. In I Cor. vii 21, does a study of the particles in the phrase ἀλλ' εἰ καὶ δύνασαι ἐλεύθερος γενέσθαι give any indication of whether Paul intends to encourage Christian slaves to take advantage of a chance of freedom or whether he is instructing them to remain slaves? And in II Cor. v 3, how does the interpretation of εἴ γε καὶ ἐνδυσάμενοι relate to the general problem of the apparent contradiction which exists within the first ten verses of the chapter?

1. *Lk. xxii 42 and Mt. xxvi 39*

The Marcan version of Jesus' prayer in the garden of Gethsemane reads: ἀββὰ ὁ πατήρ, πάντα δυνατά σοι· παρένεγκε τὸ ποτήριον τοῦτο ἀπ' ἐμοῦ· ἀλλ' οὐ τί ἐγὼ θέλω, ἀλλὰ τί σύ (Mk. xiv 36). Luke and Matthew have πλήν instead of the first Marcan ἀλλά: namely, πάτερ, εἰ βούλει, παρένεγκε τοῦτο τὸ ποτήριον ἀπ' ἐμοῦ· πλὴν μὴ τὸ θέλημά μου ἀλλὰ τὸ σὸν γινέσθω (Lk. xxii 42), and πάτερ μου, εἰ δυνατόν ἐστιν παρελθάτω ἀπ' ἐμοῦ τὸ ποτήριον τοῦτο· πλὴν οὐχ ὡς ἐγὼ θέλω, ἀλλ' ὡς σύ (Mt. xxvi 39). If ἀλλά in Mark performs its normal function as an eliminating adversative particle, its effect is to give the impression of a severe mental conflict. Since it entirely contradicts what precedes, it shows Jesus as acknowledging that the will of God is in direct opposition to his human desire to escape suffering. The conflict is sharply defined. It is necessary to consider the possibility that the use of πλήν by the other two Evangelists is intended to modify the impression of conflict which is produced by the Marcan version.

In the case of the Lucan version, however, it seems unlikely that such a modification was consciously intended. The following verses (xxii 43-44) may well be part of the original text. Creed points out that there is good manuscript authority for them and suggests that they may have been omitted in some Alexandrian texts for the same doctrinal motive which led the author of the Fourth Gospel to omit the agony and the prayer in the garden entirely. He refers to Harnack, who maintains that the verses contain character- istically Lucan language; ἐκτενῶς in connection with prayer is used again in Acts xii 5, and ἐνισχύω recurs in Acts ix 19. [1] If this argument is valid, and the longer text is to be accepted, it is plainly impossible to suppose that the Evangelist had any intention of diminishing the effect of conflict which is produced by the ac- count in Mark. Some other explanation must be found for the substitution of πλήν for ἀλλά. The second half of the verse in Luke differs considerably from the Marcan version in other respects as well, so it is possible that it was derived from a different source. [2] Whether this is so or not, it could in any case be argued that the Lucan πλήν is simply the equivalent of the Marcan ἀλλά. There are two clear instances elsewhere in Luke where πλήν performs exactly the same function as ἀλλά (xii 31; xxiii 28), and two further exam- ples where this is a tenable interpretation of the particle (vi 35; xxii 21).

There is on the other hand a high degree of probability that the Matthean version is an intentional modification of Mark. Matthew uses πλήν infrequently, [3] so that its occurrence here can scarcely be regarded as simply accidental. There is no reason to suppose that it could be derived from a separate, non-Marcan source, nor is it likely to be the equivalent of ἀλλά, as in Luke, since

---

[1] J. M. Creed, *The Gospel according to St Luke*, London, 1930, p. 273.

[2] See Vincent Taylor, *Behind the Third Gospel*, Oxford, 1926, p. 44.

[3] There are four examples in addition to the one under consideration, namely xi 22, 24; xviii 7; xxvi 64.

there are no examples of the use of πλήν in this sense in the rest of the Gospel.

There are two possibilities. The author may use πλήν as a balancing adversative particle, as in xviii 7. In that case the sense of the verse would be: "If it is possible, let me escape suffering. *Nevertheless*, the will of God, not my own desire for escape, must be the determining factor." Here the conflict is envisaged as possible, but not as inevitable. The desire to escape and the intention of doing God's will are two different, but not necessarily contradictory, attitudes of mind. The conflict between them has not, properly speaking, begun. The second possibility is that πλήν introduces a condition. This is a form of its original limitative sense, and is found several times in the Septuagint, e.g. κατὰ πάντα, ὅσα ἠκούσαμεν Μωυσῆ, ἀκουσόμεθα σοῦ, πλὴν ἔστω κύριος ὁ θεὸς ἡμῶν μετὰ σοῦ, ὃν τρόπον ἦν μετὰ Μωυσῆ (Josh. i 17). [1] If this is the function of πλήν in the Matthean prayer the verse might be paraphrased: "If it is possible, let me escape suffering, *on condition that* the will of God may still be accomplished." On this interpretation the two attitudes of mind are completely integrated, with the one subordinated to the other. There is no real conflict at all. In both cases the impression produced by the Marcan saying is considerably modified.

The fact that in the Matthean version there is a second quotation of the actual words of Jesus may be of some assistance in deciding between these two possible interpretations of πλήν. Are the two prayers intended to have an exactly identical meaning? The πάλιν ἐκ δευτέρου of verse 42 may refer only to the act of prayer, and not to its content. On the other hand, verse 44, πάλιν ἀπελθὼν προσηύξατο ἐκ τρίτου, τὸν αὐτὸν λόγον εἰπὼν πάλιν, at least suggests that the content of Jesus' prayer was the same on all three occasions. If the Evangelist intended the two prayers to mean the same thing, an examination of the second may throw some light on the precise significance of the first. The second prayer reads as follows: πάτερ μου, εἰ οὐ δύναται τοῦτο παρελθεῖν, ἐὰν μὴ αὐτὸ πίω, γενηθήτω τὸ θέλημά σου (Mt. xxvi 42). In view of Jesus' words to the crowd in verses 53-54, the δυνατόν of verse 39 and the οὐ δύναται in verse 42 must refer not to possibility in general but to the possibility or impossibility of some specific divine action within the framework of the accomplishment of God's purposes—a possibility

---

[1] Cf. Num. xxxvi 6; Jg. x 15; I King. xii 24; II King. iii 13; Jer. x 24.

and impossibility which are determined not by any external factor but by the exigencies of the divine purpose themselves. This being so, the saying may be paraphrased: "I am willing to suffer if the purposes of God require it of me." This would be the reverse side, as it were, of the first prayer, if πλήν in verse 39 introduces a condition: "Let me escape suffering, on condition that the will of God allows me to do so." If the two prayers are, in fact, meant to be identical, a conditional sense is required for πλήν. Otherwise, if verse 44 is interpreted less strictly, πλήν might be understood as a balancing adversative, and the first prayer would then tentatively suggest the possibility of a conflict, while the second would express its resolution. The moment of conflict itself would not be explicitly indicated. But it is rather doubtful whether the Evangelist could really be supposed to have had this kind of psychological progression in mind. If he were consciously attempting to express such a development from one attitude of mind to another, one would expect to find the resolution of the mental conflict expressed in the third, not the second, prayer, whereas in actual fact the content of the third prayer is not explicitly quoted, and we are merely told that it was the same as the second (and, perhaps, identical with the first). It is more likely that the second prayer was inserted to emphasize and clarify the meaning of the first. In that case, πλήν must perform a limiting, conditional function, and Matthew will have modified his source by representing as already resolved a conflict which in Mark is acutely present and immediate.

2. *Mt. xxvi* 64

Here also there is some question of whether Matthew has modified his original source. In the Marcan version of the trial before the Sanhedrin, when the High Priest asks Jesus whether he is the Christ, Jesus replies: ἐγώ εἰμι, καὶ ὄψεσθε τὸν υἱὸν τοῦ ἀνθρώπου ἐκ δεξιῶν καθήμενον τῆς δυνάμεως καὶ ἐρχόμενον μετὰ τῶν νεφελῶν τοῦ οὐρανοῦ (Mk. xiv 62). In Matthew, however, the reply reads: σὺ εἶπας· πλὴν λέγω ὑμῖν, ἀπ' ἄρτι ὄψεσθε τὸν υἱὸν τοῦ ἀνθρώπου καθήμενον ἐκ δεξιῶν τῆς δυνάμεως καὶ ἐρχόμενον ἐπὶ τῶν νεφελῶν τοῦ οὐρανοῦ. The modification, if such there is, would cause Jesus to give an evasive rather than a directly affirmative answer. There are no satisfactory external parallels which would provide a clue to the meaning of σὺ εἶπας, so that the exegesis depends to a large extent upon the function exercized by πλήν.

Probably the most frequent interpretation is to understand πλήν as adversative. [1] This is certainly its most usual function, both in the New Testament and in the κοινή in general, and it is used in this way in Mt. xviii 7. This makes the reply evasive: "That is how you would describe me. I should not myself use precisely that term (although I do not absolutely reject it). However, I do tell you that you will see the Son of Man immediately vindicated."

E. J. Goodspeed, on the other hand, would take πλήν as affirmative and progressive. [2] He maintains that "the basic meaning of πλήν (πλέον) is 'More, Nay more, Moreover, Furthermore' . . . . It is just the word Matthew felt Mark needed to introduce the great sentence about the coming of the Son of Man. There is nothing about it to suggest any weakening of Mark's affirmative, which Matthew has represented by Σὺ εἶπας." As this last sentence indicates, the result of taking πλήν as the equivalent of the Marcan progressive καί is to settle the meaning of σὺ εἶπας as a direct and unequivocal affirmative.

Both these solutions present difficulties of one sort or another. Goodspeed's appeal to etymology to determine the meaning of πλήν as used by Matthew is an extraordinarily dubious procedure. The sense he postulates was unknown to classical authors and is to all appearances without parallel in the κοινή, although there may perhaps be one or two examples of progressive πλήν in Luke as a result of the influence of the Septuagint. [3] It is possible that this influence may have been operative in Matthew as well, but, unless this can be shown, Goodspeed's interpretation of πλήν is untenable. It is highly unlikely that the Evangelist, simply on the basis of a supposed (but improbable) knowledge of the word's derivation, would have reverted to an hypothetical original use of πλήν which had been already lost sight of in the classical period.

Nevertheless, the conventional exegesis presents problems of its own. For one thing, it requires the assumption of a substantial ellipsis before πλὴν λέγω ὑμῖν. J. H. Thayer, who treats πλήν as adversative and σὺ εἶπας as evasive, paraphrases the whole verse in the following way: "That challenge by which thou wouldst make

---

[1] See A. H. McNeile, *The Gospel according to St Matthew*, London, 1915, p. 402; also W. C. Allen, *A Critical and Exegetical Commentary on the Gospel according to St Matthew*, Edinburgh, 1907, p. 284.

[2] Edgar J. Goodspeed, *Problems of New Testament Translation*, Chicago, 1945, p. 65.

[3] See above, pp. 22-23.

me criminate myself may pass. The malice in it is thine. But, setting that aside [i.e. 'Nevertheless'], I declare to thee and those whose representative thou art, that from this time on ye shall see the apocalyptic description of the Messiah becoming verified." [1] This is perhaps unnecessarily elaborate, but some addition is demanded if adversative πλήν is to make sense. Secondly, and this objection is the more important one, it is extremely difficult to find a convincing reason why Matthew should have altered the clear affirmation of messiahship which stood in his source. Morton Smith, criticizing Goodspeed, [2] claims that the Evangelist's object is "to protect Jesus from any appearance of blasphemy, and so to represent his opponents as putting him to death, without provocation, out of blind malice." But in that case, why has he retained the saying about sitting at the right hand of power? According to Billerbeck, this was the real foundation for the charge of blasphemy. [3] J. A. T. Robinson attempts to answer the second objection by adopting for Mk. xiv 62 the reading σὺ εἶπας ὅτι ἐγώ εἰμι. [4] If this reading is original, the Marcan reply is itself evasive, and Matthew has not introduced an essential modification but has simply abbreviated what he may have felt to be an unnecessarily cumbersome phrase. But the textual evidence strongly suggests that σὺ εἶπας ὅτι ἐγώ εἰμι, far from being the original text of Mark, is in fact a later conflation of Mark and Matthew. It is attested by the following witnesses: Θ 067 fam[13] 471 543 565 700 1071 Geo Arm Or. An examination of the text of the Marcan Passion Narrative shows that there are at least ten instances where two or more of these witnesses have added to the Marcan text a word or a phrase derived from the parallel verse in Matthew. [5] There is thus a strong probability that the same thing has happened at xiv 62.

Since there are objections both to Goodspeed's interpretation of the verse and to the more usual exegesis which adopts an adver-

---

[1] "Σὺ εἶπας, Σὺ λέγεις, in the Answers of Jesus," *Journal of Biblical Literature*, xiii (1894), 40-49.

[2] Morton Smith, "Notes on Goodspeed's 'Problems of New Testament Translation,' " *ibid.*, lxiv (1945), 501-514.

[3] [Strack-]Billerbeck, *Kommentar*, i, 1017.

[4] John A. T. Robinson, *Jesus and his Coming*, London, 1957, p. 49.

[5] Mk. xiv 9 (cf. Mt. xxvi 13); Mk. xiv 22 (cf. Mt. xxvi 26); Mk. xiv 24 (cf. Mt. xxvi 28); Mk. xiv 27 (cf. Mt. xxvi 31); Mk. xiv 35 (cf. Mt. xxvi 39); Mk. xiv 65 (cf. Mt. xxvi 68); Mk. xiv 70 (cf. Mt. xxvi 73); Mk. xv 17 (cf. Mt. xxvii 28); Mk. xv 20 (cf. Mt. xxvii 31); Mk. xv 23 (cf. Mt. xxvii 34).

sative sense for πλήν, it may be worthwhile to suggest a slightly different method of approach. It seems to have escaped the notice of commentators on Mt. xxvi 64 that the phrase πλὴν λέγω ὑμῖν occurs at two other points in the Gospel (Mt. xi 22, 24). The first of these two examples has a parallel at Lk. x 14; the substance of the verse is the same, and in Luke also it is introduced by the particle πλήν, although it is not followed by λέγω ὑμῖν. It has been suggested already [1] that in this saying it would be preferable to assume a continuative and progressive relation between the πλήν-sentence and the preceding one, and to translate πλήν as "moreover." The suggestion was made in connection with the version in Luke. It may be valid for the Matthean version as well, but in Matthew there is an alternative possibility which is brought to light as a result of a comparison between xi 24 and its doublet in x 15. It will be convenient to set out the relevant evidence in more detail.

Matthew	*Luke*
x 15 ἀμὴν λέγω ὑμῖν, ἀνεκτό- τερον ἔσται	x 12 λέγω ὑμῖν ὅτι Σοδόμοις ἐν τῇ
γῇ Σοδόμων καὶ Γομόρρων ἐν ἡμέ- ρᾳ κρίσεως ἢ τῇ πόλει ἐκείνῃ.	ἡμέρᾳ ἐκείνῃ ἀνεκτότερον ἔσται ἢ τῇ πόλει ἐκείνῃ.
xi 22 πλὴν λέγω ὑμῖν, Τύρῳ καὶ Σιδῶνι ἀνεκτότερον ἔσται ἐν ἡμέρᾳ κρίσεως ἢ ὑμῖν.	x 14 πλὴν Τύρῳ καὶ Σιδῶνι ἀνεκ- τότερον ἔσται ἐν τῇ κρίσει ἢ ὑμῖν.

xi 24 πλὴν λέγω ὑμῖν ὅτι γῇ Σοδόμων ἀνεκτότερον ἔσται ἐν ἡμέρᾳ κρίσεως ἢ σοί.

In the first saying, ἀμήν has been either added by Matthew or omitted by Luke. In the second saying the introductory πλήν would appear to have been contained in the source. The third saying as a whole may perhaps have stood in the source as well and have been omitted by Luke as superfluous, or it may be a Matthean repetition. In any case, the occurrence of πλήν is not primarily due to Matthew himself. This raises the question of how he understood the particle when he found it in his source, and the existence of the phrase ἀμὴν λέγω ὑμῖν at the beginning of a saying

---

[1] See above, pp. 22-23.

almost identical with those in xi 22, 24 suggests that there is at least a possibility that he may have thought of it as an asseverative, adverbial particle, the equivalent of ἀμήν, rather than as a connective. If ἀμήν stood in his source as well as one (or both) of the πλήν-sayings, the equivalence of the sayings may have led to his equating the meaning of the introductory particles. If, on the other hand, ἀμήν is the Evangelist's own addition, the fact that he has used it at the beginning of a saying closely similar to those which are later introduced by πλήν may indicate that he read πλήν in these sayings as the equivalent of ἀμήν and so thought ἀμήν suitable to introduce x 15. The prior possibility of treating πλήν as adverbial and emphatic derives from its use in the Septuagint to translate the Hebrew asseverative אַךְ. Since in Mt. xxvi 39 πλήν is used in a sense which is found several times in the Septuagint, it is not improbable that the Septuagintal idiom may have influenced the Evangelist's interpretation of his source for xi 22. If, then, there is some justification for treating πλὴν λέγω ὑμῖν in Mt. xi 22, 24 as equivalent to ἀμὴν λέγω ὑμῖν, it is possible to argue that the phrase means the same thing when it occurs at xxvi 64. It would give the sense which Goodspeed feels to be necessary, and, at the same time, the derivation of this use of πλήν from the Septuagint would provide a sounder exegetical basis than Goodspeed's appeal to etymology. The great advantage of interpreting πλήν in this way is that we are relieved of the necessity of finding a reason for the Matthean alteration of Mark, which must be supposed to have taken place if πλήν is read as adversative. If the saying about the vindication of the Son of Man is simply a stronger affirmation of the preceding σὺ εἶπας, then σὺ εἶπας itself must be regarded as a straightforward affirmative, and the equivalent of the Marcan ἐγώ εἰμι.

There are, however, three objections to this interpretation of σὺ εἶπας which must be considered, since, if they are valid, they will cast doubts upon the suggested exegesis of πλήν. First, it has been maintained that the pronoun in the phrase should be given its full emphasis, in which case Jesus' answer must mean: "The term is yours, not mine." Secondly, it is possible that σὺ εἶπας is the equivalent of ὑμεῖς λέγετε in Lk. xxii 70 and of σὺ λέγεις in Mk. xv 2 and Jn. xviii 37, and these replies are not affirmative but non-committal. Thirdly, the σὺ εἶπας in Mt. xxvi 25 (Jesus' reply to Judas) may be intended as an ambiguous answer.

(a) The first objection is the least convincing. Thayer supposes that the σύ in the reply to the High Priest echoes the σύ in the preceding question and that some emphasis attaches to it on this account. But this would be a tenable argument only if the pronoun in both question and reply had the same reference, i.e. occurred in parallel clauses as the subject of the same verb. If the High Priest had said to Jesus: ἐξορκίζω σε . . . ἵνα σὺ ἡμῖν εἴπῃς, εἰ σὺ εἶ ὁ Χριστός, then it might be reasonable to suppose that some emphasis belonged to the pronoun in the reply σὺ εἶπας. As it is, the occurrence of σύ in non-parallel phrases in the two sentences does not necessarily give an impression of emphasis. Nor are the two occurrences in the question in any sense emphatic; the verb ἐξορκίζω requires an object, which σε supplies, and in the last clause the emphasis lies on ὁ Χριστός (there is no question here of other claimants to the title). There is therefore no compelling reason to emphasize σύ in σὺ εἶπας.

(b) The second argument is more substantial. In the Lucan version of the trial before the Sanhedrin the whole assembly say to Jesus, σὺ οὖν εἶ ὁ υἱὸς τοῦ θεοῦ; and he replies, ὑμεῖς λέγετε ὅτι ἐγώ εἰμι (Lk. xxii 70). In the Johannine account of the trial before Pilate there is a similar reply when Pilate asks Jesus whether he is a king; Jesus answers, σὺ λέγεις ὅτι βασιλεύς εἰμι (Jn. xviii 37). The same question in the Marcan version is answered simply with the phrase σὺ λέγεις. All three replies are probably intentionally ambiguous. Thayer points out that the ὅτι-clauses in the first two are tautologous and difficult to make sense of if ὑμεῖς λέγετε and σὺ λέγεις mean simply "Yes." He also remarks that if, in Mk. xv 2, Jesus openly agrees that he is the King of the Jews, it is very strange that Pilate professes to find no fault in him and makes every effort to release him. Thus, if σὺ εἶπας is the equivalent of σὺ λέγεις, it is probably evasive and non-committal. Goodspeed, however, while accepting the equivalence of the phrases, disagrees with Thayer's interpretation of σὺ λέγεις and ὑμεῖς λέγετε, and maintains that these too are direct affirmatives. [1] In Lk. xxii 70-71 σὺ λέγεις is shown to be such by the questioners' response to it. And in Jn. xviii 37 Jesus "can hardly fail to admit that he is a king when he has just been talking about his kingdom." He further asserts that important evidence on the meaning of σὺ λέγεις and the origin of

---

[1] *Op. cit.*, pp. 64-68.

the idiom is afforded by a question and reply in the *Oedipus Tyrannus* of Sophocles, where someone says λέγω τι; ("Am I right?") and receives the straightforward affirmative answer: λέγεις (*O.T.* 1475-76).

The first two points, however, are inconclusive, and the third incorrect. The result of the trial before the Sanhedrin was pretty well a foregone conclusion, and Jesus' accusers may easily have accepted a non-committal reply as an affirmative one. In the Johannine account of the trial before Pilate, the explanation of an evasive answer in xviii 37 is probably that Pilate and Jesus mean different things by kingship, so that the latter is unable to reply to the question with an unqualified affirmative. Lastly, it is hardly safe to maintain that a single quotation from classical Greek drama is decisive evidence for New Testament and κοινή usage, and in any case the quotation's linguistic significance is misinterpreted. The word λέγεις may express assent here, but it does so by virtue of the common Greek idiom which indicates agreement by means of the repetition of a key-word from the previous speech. There are numerous examples; e.g. ἀλλὰ μὴν ὁμολογοῦμεν, ᾧ γε ὅμοιος ἑκάτερος εἴη, τοιοῦτον καὶ ἑκάτερον εἶναι. ὁμολογοῦμεν γάρ (Pl. *R.* 350 C); οὐ διοίσονται καὶ μισήσουσι καὶ ἐχθροὶ ἔσονται ἀλλήλοις τε καὶ τοῖς δικαίοις; ἔσονται, ἔφη (*ibid.* 351 E).[1] The quotation from Sophocles conforms to this pattern, and is no evidence for the use of λέγεις as an affirmative answer where λέγειν has not been used by the previous speaker. Also, it is very doubtful whether the verb λέγειν by itself can mean "to be right"; when used in this sense it requires to be supplemented by such words as τι, εὖ, καλῶς, or ὀρθῶς. Moreover, Goodspeed's suggested translations of Lk. xxii 70 and Jn. xviii 37 would seem to show that he is himself slightly uncertain about the force of his own argument. He would translate Lk. xxii 70 by "I am, as you say," and Jn. xviii 37 by "As you say, I am a king." [2] These renderings indicate that he really regards the affirmative force of the answers as inhering not in the ὑμεῖς λέγετε and σὺ λέγεις but in the following ἐγώ εἰμι. It is therefore better to reject Goodspeed's arguments and to follow Thayer in regarding σὺ λέγεις and ὑμεῖς λέγετε as ambiguous.

But is it absolutely certain that σὺ εἶπας is the exact equivalent of these expressions, and so must also be regarded as ambiguous?

---

[1] Cf. 353 A, D, E.
[2] *Op. cit.*, pp. 66-67.

Surely the difference in tense suggests that there may be a difference in meaning. The aorist tense gives to σὺ εἶπας a definiteness which is lacking in σὺ λέγεις, and thus makes it less likely that the phrase is evasive or indirect. There is a similar difference in tense and implication between our "You've said it" and "So you say." The present tense in σὺ λέγεις may well imply: "That is the way you (habitually) speak of it," i.e. "That is your attitude towards the matter (I should not myself put it in quite the same terms)." By contrast, σὺ εἶπας will mean: "You have (this minute) made the decisive statement," which would presumably imply: "You are right." Thus, the supposed parallels to σὺ εἶπας in the other three Gospels may not in fact prove of much use in determining its meaning. The only really safe guide is the previous occurrence of the identical phrase in Matthew itself. This brings us to the third objection.

(c) Morton Smith claims that σὺ εἶπας in the reply to Judas (Mt. xxvi 25) must be indirect and ambiguous, "for if Jesus had told Judas plainly that he knew he was about to betray him, the betrayal would presumably have stopped." It is doubtful, however, whether an inconsistency of this kind would have worried the Evangelist. There is a similar difficulty in the Johannine account of the handing of the sop to Judas (Jn. xiii 23-30). At least one of the disciples is informed of the identity of the traitor, and Judas himself is made aware of the fact that Jesus knows his intentions, but the betrayal nevertheless takes place. It is also necessary to consider the reason for Matthew's expansion of the Marcan narrative at this point. In view of his general dependence upon Mark in the Passion Narrative it is highly improbable that he possessed any authentic additional information about the conversation between Jesus and his disciples concerning the betrayal. One cannot, therefore, argue in favor of the ambiguity of σὺ εἶπας on the grounds that the question and answer are a piece of genuine historical reminiscence and that Jesus is unlikely to have given a direct reply to Judas since, in that case, the other disciples would have prevented Judas's subsequent action. It is more likely that the motive for the addition was of a doctrinal character. It may have been the Evangelist's intention to show that Jesus had an accurate foreknowledge of what was to happen to him, including the knowledge of the identity of his betrayer. The author of the Fourth Gospel makes this point explicitly (Jn. xiii 11), and it may have been an element in the thought of the Church as a whole, and not simply a Johannine characteristic. If this is the motive for the insertion of Judas's question and Jesus' reply in the Matthean account of the Last Supper, σὺ εἶπας must be understood as an unequivocal affirmative.

It would appear from the preceding discussion that the objections to interpreting σὺ εἶπας as directly affirmative are unconvincing, that the aorist tense strongly suggests that this is its function, and finally that it is in all probability a formula of straightforward assent in Mt. xxvi 25.

The occurrence of σὺ εἶπας in Mt. xxvi 64 is therefore no hindrance to understanding the following πλήν as asseverative. We may conclude that the Matthean reply to the High Priest is simply a stronger version of the answer which the Evangelist found in Mark, and that it means: "Yes, I am. Indeed I tell you that you will see me immediately vindicated."

3. *I Cor. vii* 21

The problem here is whether a Christian slave with the opportunity of emancipation is to take advantage of the opportunity or to refuse it. Paul's words are ambiguous: δοῦλος ἐκλήθης; μή σοι μελέτω· ἀλλ' εἰ καὶ δύνασαι ἐλεύθερος γενέσθαι, μᾶλλον χρῆσαι. The ambiguity arises from the fact that the object of χρῆσαι must be supplied from the rest of the sentence. In itself this is a perfectly legitimate usage. C. H. Dodd [1] has drawn attention to a similar use of χρῆσαι in one of the papyri: καὶ πολλάκις ἐξ[ῆν γράψαι σοι περὶ τοῦ] κεφαλαίου τούτου, καὶ προσδοκον (*leg.* προσδοκῶν) καθ' ἑκάστην καταλαμβά[νειν ἐκεῖσε], τούτου ἕνεκεν οὐκ ἐχρησάμην ἄλλην γράψαι ἄλλοις γράμμα[σι]ν (P. Oxy. XVI 1865, 4 ff.). The editors translate this as follows: "I had many opportunities of writing to you concerning this matter, and expecting each day to come thither, for that reason did not avail myself of them to write another letter over again."

Dodd comments that the object of χρῆσαι is supplied from ἐξῆν, and maintains that the Pauline instance is an exact parallel, in which the object is to be supplied from the sense of δύνασαι, so that the verse may be translated: "If you actually have before you the possibility of becoming free, avail yourself of it by preference." This second assertion, however, is less convincing. In the papyrus

---

[1] "Notes from Papyri," *Journal of Theological Studies*, xxvi (1924), 77-78.

there is only one possible object which the rest of the sentence provides for χρῆσαι, but in the Pauline example the difficulty consists precisely in the fact that two different, and conflicting, objects are possible. Dodd favors δύνασαι, but it could equally well be maintained that the object is to be supplied from the sense of the preceding δοῦλος ἐκλήθης, which gives an entirely opposite meaning. Opinions of exegetes are divided. Rengstorf, writing on δοῦλος in the Kittel *Wörterbuch*, [1] thinks that Paul intends the slave to take advantage of his opportunity of emancipation, and so would refer back to δύνασαι to supply the missing object, but Schlier, writing on ἐλεύθερος, prefers to supply δουλεία. [2]

In view of this diversity of opinion, it is worth considering whether the introductory particles at the beginning of the second half of the verse throw any light on the interpretation of their context. If εἰ and καί are combined to mean "although" or "even if," [3] then it would seem more natural to supply δουλεία as the object of χρῆσαι, but if they are separated, so that καί becomes emphatic and modifies either δύνασαι or the phrase as a whole, it would be possible to understand ἐλευθερία as the omitted object.

Pauline usage in general provides parallel examples of both idioms. There are several instances of the combination εἰ καί in the sense of "although"; e.g. ὅτι εἰ καὶ ἐλύπησα ὑμᾶς ἐν τῇ ἐπιστολῇ, οὐ μεταμέλομαι (II Cor. vii 8a) and εἰ γὰρ καὶ τῇ σαρκὶ ἄπειμι, ἀλλὰ τῷ πνεύματι σὺν ὑμῖν εἰμι (Col. ii 5). In the following verse, as in I Cor. vii 21, εἰ καί is preceded by ἀλλά: thus διὸ οὐκ ἐγκακοῦμεν· ἀλλ' εἰ καὶ ὁ ἔξω ἡμῶν ἄνθρωπος διαφθείρεται, ἀλλ' ὁ ἔσω ἡμῶν ἀνακαινοῦται ἡμέρα καὶ ἡμέρᾳ (II Cor. iv 16).

It is not always easy to distinguish between "although" and "even if." In the following examples, "even if" would make good sense, although the meaning "although" is not excluded: οὐδὲν γὰρ ὑστέρησα τῶν ὑπερλίαν ἀποστόλων, εἰ καὶ οὐδέν εἰμι (II Cor. xii 11), and βλέπω ὅτι ἡ ἐπιστολὴ ἐκείνη εἰ καὶ πρὸς ὥραν ἐλύπησεν ὑμᾶς (II Cor. vii 8c).

There are also a number of examples in which καί is used emphatically in the protasis of a conditional sentence, and so is separated grammatically from εἰ: thus τί δὲ ἔχεις ὃ οὐκ ἔλαβες; εἰ δὲ καὶ ἔλαβες,

---

[1] K. H. Rengstorf, δοῦλος, *Theologisches Wörterbuch zum Neuen Testament* (edit. Gerhard Kittel), II, Stuttgart, 1935, 274-275.

[2] H. Schlier, *op. cit.*, p. 498.

[3] See Denn., pp. 299-302.

τί καυχᾶσαι ὡς μὴ λαβών; (I Cor. iv 7), τοῖς δὲ γεγαμηκόσιν παραγγέλλω, οὐκ ἐγώ, ἀλλὰ ὁ κύριος, γυναῖκα ἀπὸ ἀνδρὸς μὴ χωρισθῆναι, — ἐὰν δὲ καὶ χωρισθῇ, μενέτω ἄγαμος, . . . (I Cor. vii 10-11), λέλυσαι ἀπὸ γυναικός; μὴ ζήτει γυναῖκα. ἐὰν δὲ καὶ γαμήσῃς, οὐχ ἥμαρτες (I Cor. vii 27-28), and ἀλλὰ τῇ φανερώσει τῆς ἀληθείας συνιστάνοντες ἑαυτοὺς πρὸς πᾶσαν συνείδησιν ἀνθρώπων ἐνώπιον τοῦ θεοῦ. εἰ δὲ καὶ ἔστιν κεκαλυμμένον τὸ εὐαγγέλιον ἡμῶν, ἐν τοῖς ἀπολλυμένοις ἐστὶν κεκαλυμμένον (II Cor. iv 2-3); possibly also λογίζομαι γὰρ μηδὲν ὑστερηκέναι τῶν ὑπερλίαν ἀποστόλων. εἰ δὲ καὶ ἰδιώτης τῷ λόγῳ, ἀλλ' οὐ τῇ γνώσει (II Cor. xi 5-6), and οὐ μεταμέλομαι· εἰ καὶ μετεμελόμην . . . νῦν χαίρω (II Cor. vii 8b-9).

Most of these examples reveal a common pattern. In five out of the six an adversative δέ follows the subordinating particle, and in four instances (I Cor. iv 7; vii 11, 27-28; II Cor. vii 8b) the word emphasized by καί constitutes a repetition, or virtual repetition, of some word in the preceding sentence. This is a pattern which occurs several times in Epictetus, e.g. οὐκοῦν πρῶτον μὲν οὐκ ἂν ἐγένετο Ἡρακλῆς ἐν τρυφῇ τοιαύτῃ καὶ ἡσυχίᾳ νυστάζων ὅλον τὸν βίον· εἰ δ' ἄρα καὶ ἐγένετο, τί ὄφελος αὐτοῦ; (Dss. I 6, 33). [1] In II Cor. iv 3 and xi 6 the pattern is altered a little. The word or phrase emphasized by καί is not a repetition from the previous sentence but the direct opposite of one of its key expressions. Thus, in the first instance κεκαλυμμένος is opposed to the preceding φανέρωσις, and in the second ἰδιώτης τῷ λόγῳ seems to be contrasted with μηδὲν ὑστερηκέναι. This form of the pattern also has parallels elsewhere; e.g. τοῖς ἀρετὴν διαπονοῦσι . . . περιέσται τὸ εἰς ἅπαν ἄνοσον· εἰ δὲ καὶ γένοιτό τις ἀσθένεια. . . . (Philo, de Praem. xx), and κενὴν δὲ μαχίμων λογιζόμενος εἶναι τὴν πόλιν ὁ Τραϊανός, εἰ δὲ καί τινες ἔνδον εἶεν. . . . (Joseph. de Bell. Jud. III 298). If the verse under consideration fits into the pattern, it is this second form to which it will belong; καί may stress the whole phrase δύνασαι ἐλεύθερος γενέσθαι, which will be opposed to the preceding δοῦλος ἐκλήθης, or it may emphasize δύνασαι alone, in which case the idea of being offered one's freedom will be contrasted with that of seeking it by one's own efforts, implied in μή σοι μελέτω. It deviates, however, from the pattern as seen elsewhere, in that the connecting particle is not δέ but ἀλλά. This might mean that it is not an example of the idiom at all, and that the alternative interpretation of εἰ καί as "although"

---

[1] Cf. III 23, 18; IV 13, 17-19.

is to be preferred. On the other hand, a comparison with the two other instances in the same chapter suggests a possible explanation of the difference. In I Cor. vii 11 and 27-28 the previous sentence expresses the ideal situation, in one case the faithful preservation of the marriage relationship, in the other the maintenance of the celibate state by the unmarried, while the following conditional protasis introduced by δέ describes an alternative possibility which is permissible but not ideal, divorce on the part of the married and marriage for the celibate. But the alternative possibility is not to be regarded as in any sense negating or weakening the force of the previous injunctions to faithfulness and to celibacy. Likewise, in II Cor. iv 3 the fact that to some the truth of the Gospel remains unrevealed does not invalidate the complementary truth that to others it is being made plain. In these instances δέ is the correct particle to express the relationship between the sentences, since it is a balancing adversative which suggests a divergent possibility rather than an eliminating particle which denies the validity of what has gone before. In I Cor. vii 21, however, a balancing adversative might be thought out of place. Paul could hardly have regarded the state of slavery as an ideal condition. The possibility of freedom might thus be considered to negate completely his previous advice not to worry about being a slave. And in that case the right particle to use would be ἀλλά, not δέ. The deviation from the normal pattern would therefore be logically required by the context.

The main problem of exegesis remains unresolved. All that the preceding evidence has shown is that Pauline usage in general would provide support both for understanding εἰ καί as "although" and for separating καί from εἰ and treating it as emphatic. There is, however, one factor which might suggest that the second alternative is to be preferred. An examination of the whole chapter in which the advice to slaves occurs shows that it contains no examples of εἰ καί meaning "although" or "even if," but has two instances of an emphatic καί in a conditional protasis (I Cor. vii 11, 28), one before and one after the verse under consideration. It is therefore probable that this verse contains a third example of the idiom. This would mean that Paul is advising Christian slaves to take advantage of the opportunity of emancipation. Two further linguistic arguments in support of this interpretation are suggested by H. L. Goudge. He points out first that since it is necessary to supply an object for χρῆσαι it is much simpler to understand a repetition of the immediately preceding ἐλεύθερος γενέσθαι than to supply δουλεία from the rather more remote δοῦλος ἐκλήθης, and secondly that the aorist tense of χρῆσαι indicates that Paul "has in mind a single decisive action, such as the acceptance of an offered freedom would be." [1]

Schlier would object to this interpretation for the following reasons. First, in the next verse (presumably intended as explanatory of μᾶλλον χρῆσαι) Paul points out that as regards their relationship to Christ there is no difference in status between slaves and those who are free. Secondly, the apostle goes on to warn his readers of the consequences of striving after external freedom; by making claims of this sort they will become slaves to a purely human and worldly way of looking at things. Schlier would therefore prefer to supply δουλεία as the omitted object. His first point has some force. But it is possible to regard the whole conditional sentence as a parenthesis, as in the parallel example in verses 10-11, and in that case the γάρ-clause of verse 22 would be explanatory not of μᾶλλον χρῆσαι but of μή σοι μελέτω, and so would not affect the meaning of verse 21b. The second argument depends upon a somewhat strained and over-subtle exegesis of verse 23b, μὴ γίνεσθε δοῦλοι ἀνθρώπων. This can surely be taken quite literally and used in support of the alternative interpretation of verse 21, which has been shown to be preferable on linguistic grounds.

4. II Cor. v 1-10

This section of II Corinthians appears to contain within itself a fundamental contradiction. In verse 8 the death of Christians before the *Parousia* is described as ἐνδημῆσαι πρὸς τὸν κύριον, and the condition this implies is regarded by Paul as preferable to his present state, which in verse 6 he has described as ἐκδημεῖν ἀπὸ τοῦ κυρίου. In the first four verses of the chapter, however, the attitude towards the death of the individual Christian appears to be entirely different. Christians long for the replacement of their present earthly bodies by the οἰκητήριον from heaven, but are nevertheless troubled by the fear that when their physical bodies are dissolved in death they may exist in an intermediate state of "nakedness," a condition which they dread. This fear of the intermediate state is specifically expressed in verses 3-4: εἴ γε καὶ ἐνδυσάμενοι οὐ γυμνοὶ

---

[1] *The First Epistle to the Corinthians*, London 1903, pp. 58-59.

εὑρεθησόμεθα. καὶ γὰρ οἱ ὄντες ἐν τῷ σκήνει στενάζομεν βαρούμενοι, ἐφ' ᾧ οὐ θέλομεν ἐκδύσασθαι ἀλλ' ἐπενδύσασθαι, ἵνα καταποθῇ τὸ θνητὸν ὑπὸ τῆς ζωῆς.

The various attempts at resolving the contradiction are all to some extent unsatisfactory. A. Oepke [1] maintains that γυμνός refers not to the temporary condition of believers dying before the *Parousia* but to the final destiny of unbelievers for whom there is no heavenly body, so that verses 3 and 8 refer neither to the same people nor to the same state. He supports his exegesis of γυμνός by pointing out that the damned are represented as naked in the Samaritan Liturgy for the eve of the Day of Atonement. This theory has been criticized by J. N. Sevenster [2] on the grounds that the evidence

---

[1] In Kittel's *Wörterbuch*, I, Stuttgart, 1933, γυμνός, p. 774.

[2] "Some Remarks on the γυμνός in II Cor. v 3," *Studia Paulina* (edit. J. N. Sevenster and W. C. van Unnik), Haarlem, 1953, pp. 202-214. His second criticism of Oepke is unconvincing. He maintains that Oepke's theory supposes that the wicked do not rise in any general resurrection of the dead, and that this supposition is incorrect, since there are several passages where Paul assumes the definite judgment of all men, believers and unbelievers, and therefore the resurrection of the unbelievers as well as the believers (II Cor. v 10; I Thess. iv 6; Rom. xiv 10, 12; Gal. v 19-21; I Cor. vi 9 f.; II Cor. xi 14 f.; Rom. vi 21; Phil. iii 19). Two of these passages, however, may be concerned only with the judgment of believers (II Cor. v 10; Rom. xiv 10, 12). In the others, all that Paul actually says is that God will judge the evil-doers (I Thess. iv 6; II Cor. xi 14-15), that they will not inherit the Kingdom of God (Gal. v 19-21; I Cor. vi 9), and that their end is θάνατος and ἀπωλεία (Rom. vi 21; Phil. iii 19). There is no specific mention of resurrection. And the only verses which do treat of a general resurrection (I Cor. xv 21-24) suggest that it will in fact be a resurrection of believers, when the whole human race who have sinned and died in Adam are ultimately incorporated into Christ, and so are made to live. There is therefore no evidence in the Pauline Epistles for Sevenster's theory of a resurrection of unbelievers as such, and his criticism of Oepke is in this respect without foundation. It is true that the author of Acts depicts Paul as speaking of a resurrection δικαίων τε καὶ ἀδίκων (Acts xxiv 15), but it would be unsafe to assume that this is a completely accurate representation of his point of view, since it appears to contradict the impression produced by his own writings.

Substantially the same criticism is made by R. F. Hettlinger, "2 Corinthians 5 1-10," *Scottish Journal of Theology*, x (1957), 174-194, who thinks that the passages quoted by Sevenster do not necessarily refer to the judgment of the wicked dead, but can be explained as references to the judgment on sinners alive at the *Parousia*. He also asserts that "later Jewish thought had more and more approximated the conception of the lower part of Hades (as a temporary state prior to judgment) to that of Gehenna (as a final state after judgment)—a tendency which must have made it logically difficult to maintain the significance for the wicked dead of a final Judgment at the end of the Age." He quotes Plummer, Charles, and Stevens for the view that Paul did not believe in a resurrection of the wicked for judgment.

adduced by Oepke is insufficient to prove the existence here of an idea which does not occur elsewhere in the Pauline writings. Sevenster's own view, however, is equally unsatisfactory since the solution he proposes fails to recognize the real nature of the problem. He maintains that the difficulty in referring γυμνός to the state of the believer between death and resurrection is that here it is a state which Paul shrinks from, whereas in Phil. i 23 he looks forward to it. The answer to this is that the point of comparison is different; in Philippians the state in question is compared with his life on earth, whereas in II Corinthians it is compared with the putting on of the body of the resurrection. But the difficulty is not, as he implies, simply that of the contrast between II Corinthians and Philippians, but derives from the contrast between two apparently conflicting attitudes within II Corinthians v itself. [1]

Another solution has been suggested by L. Brun. [2] As in Oepke's theory, the difficulty is resolved by dissociating the state of existence described as γυμνός from the ἐνδημῆσαι πρὸς τὸν κύριον of verse 8. Brun would accept the interpretation of γυμνός which refers the term to the interim condition of those who die before the *Parousia*, but asserts that ἐνδημῆσαι πρὸς τὸν κύριον refers to the process ἐπενδύσασθαι at the *Parousia* itself, so that the following ἐνδημοῦντες describes the Christian's heavenly existence. Thus, there would be no reason to suppose that Paul would welcome the prospect of death before the *Parousia*, and so there is no conflict with the sentiments expressed in verses 3-4. This solution is likewise unconvincing. The natural way of reading ἐνδημοῦντες and ἐκδημοῦντες in verse 9 is to suppose that they are both prior to the judgment which is mentioned in the following verse, and the judgment itself presumably takes place at the *Parousia* (it is in any case inconceivable that it should be thought of as happening afterwards). It is therefore impossible to understand ἐνδημοῦντες as referring to the heavenly existence of Christians after the *Parousia*. Some commentators, in view of the difficulty of reconciling verses 3-4 with verse 8, take refuge in the supposition that the apostle simply underwent a change of mood or a change of mind between writing verses 3-4 and passing on to the rest of the chapter. [3]

---

[1] Cf. Hettlinger, p. 177, n. 1.

[2] "Zur Auslegung von II Cor. 5 1-10," *Zeitschrift für die neutestamentliche Wissenschaft*, xxviii (1929), 207-229.

[3] See Hettlinger's article, pp. 175-176.

But this is a confession of exegetical despair. Moreover, on this showing Paul must have changed his mind not once but twice within the space of ten verses, for the first verse seems to express the same kind of confidence in the face of physical death which is expressed in verse 8 but appears to be denied in verses 3-4.

The interpretation of the passage offered by R. F. Hettlinger [1] presents a more coherent and consistent exegesis, but does so at the cost of neglecting or passing over one of the major elements in the problem. Hettlinger maintains that the clothing with the spiritual body which is spoken of in verse 2 is something which takes place at the death of the individual Christian, not a process which must wait until the *Parousia*. There is therefore no possibility of an interval of disembodiment, and no contradiction in the earlier verses of the preference for death which is expressed in verse 8. The crucial verses 3-4 he would translate as follows: "on the assumption *of course* that when we shall have put on this clothing *at death* we shall not be found naked *before God*—for indeed, we who are in this tent groan, being burdened *with the pains and limitations of the physical body, but this is* not because we want to be unclothed *like the Greeks,* but *because we want* to be clothed upon, so that what is mortal may be swallowed up by life." This translation, however, is open to the objection that the problem of disembodiment is disposed of at the expense of linguistic accuracy. Hettlinger himself admits that his rendering of ἐφ᾽ ᾧ οὐ θέλομεν is, strictly speaking, incorrect, since it should really mean "because we do not want," and not "not because we want," and if we adopt the former, correct, placing of the negative, then we seem bound to regard the βαρούμενοι of the preceding clause as indicating depression caused by the fear of disembodiment. Moreover, he offers no linguistic evidence for his interpretation of εἴ γε καί as expressing assurance. He quotes Plummer's translation, "of course, on the supposition that being clothed we shall not be found naked," [2] but, despite the slightly ambiguous words he uses to translate the introductory particles, it is clear from his comments that Plummer himself regards εἴ γε as expressing not assurance but doubt. This is the interpretation favored also by J. A. T. Robinson, who describes verse 3 as a "nagging afterthought" which qualifies the hope ex-

---

[1] See above, p. 83 n. 2.
[2] Alfred Plummer, *A Critical and Exegetical Commentary on the Second Epistle of St Paul to the Corinthians,* Edinburgh, 1915, p. 147.

pressed in the preceding verse. [1] A further objection to Hettlinger's exegesis of verse 3 is that the metaphor of clothing and nakedness is found nowhere else in the New Testament in association with the idea of justification, and if we omit from his paraphrase the words "before God," the rest of it becomes impossibly tautologous and superfluous: there is no point in remarking that having put on clothing we assume we shall not be naked!

Since part, at any rate, of the problem which the chapter presents is concerned with the interpretation of the εἴ γε clause which forms verse 3, it is possible that a more detailed study of these introductory particles may throw some light on the exegesis of the whole section. We have seen already that there are two divergent views of the function of the combination εἴ γε, one which regards it as expressing assurance, the other as indicating doubt.

There are three arguments in favor of this second alternative:

(a) The general function of γε in the protasis of a conditional sentence may tend to suggest that there is some doubt as to the truth of the fact or idea which the whole sentence expresses. Denniston would translate εἴ γε as "if, but not unless." [2] The force of γε is to show that the apodosis is true only if the protasis is true—otherwise it is not true at all. In this way the particle serves to emphasize the conditionality of the whole proposition and so to cast doubts on its validity.

(b) The other Pauline example of εἴ γε followed by καί introduces a clause which is of doubtful validity: [3] ἐναρξάμενοι πνεύματι νῦν σαρκὶ ἐπιτελεῖσθε; τοσαῦτα ἐπάθετε εἰκῇ; εἴ γε καὶ εἰκῇ (Gal. iii 4). Paul hopes that the situation described in the conditional clause is not true. We might paraphrase, "I talk to you like this only on the supposition that your sufferings *were* futile; I hope they were not." Now if in Galatians this idiom is used to describe a situation which the writer hopes may not actually exist, it is quite possible that he might use it in II Corinthians to introduce a condition which he fears may not be fulfilled. In either case εἴ γε would express doubt.

(c) In II Cor. v 3 the reading εἴπερ, instead of εἴ γε, is attested by P⁴⁶BDG. The sense of εἴπερ is "if really," and according to Jebb

---

[1] John A. T. Robinson, *The Body* (*Studies in Biblical Theology* No. 5), London, 1952, p. 77.

[2] P. 223.

[3] Cf. Robinson, *op. cit.*, p. 77 n. 1.

its tone is usually confident. [1] Denniston accepts Jebb's statement with qualifications; he points to one or two classical references where εἴπερ is clearly sceptical. [2] But from the point of view of choosing the more confident of the two combinations εἴ γε and εἴπερ, it is εἴπερ which would be chosen to express assurance and εἴ γε which would appear the less confident. It is likely, therefore, that the reading εἴπερ is a reviser's attempt to deal with the apparent contradiction which verse 3 presents when considered in relation to verse 8. And this, in turn, implies that the original εἴ γε was understood as expressing doubt.

On the other hand, there are several considerations which suggest that it might be possible after all to interpret εἴ γε as indicating assurance:

(a) It is worth noticing first that Paul frequently employs the conditional form to express ideas which are not in the least hypothetical or tentative. In these cases the protasis states an accomplished fact, recognized by Paul's readers as such, and the apodosis draws a further conclusion from it. The protasis is really the equivalent of a causal clause. There are several instances in Romans, e.g. εἰ δὲ ἀπεθάνομεν σὺν Χριστῷ, πιστεύομεν ὅτι καὶ συζήσομεν αὐτῷ (Rom. vi 8), and εἰ γὰρ ἐχθροὶ ὄντες κατηλλάγημεν τῷ θεῷ . . . πολλῷ μᾶλλον καταλλαγέντες σωθησόμεθα (Rom. v 10; cf. also Rom. v 15, 17; xi 21, 24). In most of these examples it would have been equally suitable to have introduced the protasis by ἐπειδή. It is interesting to note that in I Cor. xv 21 the correlation between the results of the sin of Adam and the effects of the saving work of Christ is expressed in a causal sentence: ἐπειδὴ γὰρ δι' ἀνθρώπου θάνατος, καὶ δι' ἀνθρώπου ἀνάστασις νεκρῶν. In Rom. v, however, it is twice expressed in a conditional sentence: εἰ γὰρ τῷ τοῦ ἑνὸς παραπτώματι οἱ πολλοὶ ἀπέθανον, πολλῷ μᾶλλον ἡ χάρις τοῦ θεοῦ καὶ ἡ δωρεὰ ἐν χάριτι τῇ τοῦ ἑνὸς ἀνθρώπου Ἰησοῦ Χριστοῦ εἰς τοὺς πολλοὺς ἐπερίσσευσεν (Rom. v 15; cf. 17).

(b) Apart from Gal. iii 4, the other examples of εἴ γε in the Pauline writings would appear from their contexts to be confident rather than doubtful. In Colossians the combination stands at the beginning of a clause which, according to other remarks in the same letter, may be presumed to express the truth about the future condition of the readers: παραστῆσαι ὑμᾶς ἁγίους καὶ ἀμώμους καὶ

---

[1] See Denn., p. 487.
[2] P. 488 n. 1.

ἀνεγκλήτους κατενώπιον αὐτοῦ· εἴ γε ἐπιμένετε τῇ πίστει τεθεμελιω-μένοι καὶ ἑδραῖοι (Col. i 22-23). The implication here seems to be, "At any rate if you stand firm in the faith—and I am sure that you will"; cf. ii 5, χαίρων καὶ βλέπων ὑμῶν τὴν τάξιν, καὶ τὸ στερέωμα τῆς εἰς Χριστὸν πίστεως ὑμῶν.

There are two further examples in Ephesians. If this letter is not the work of Paul himself, they might perhaps serve as an illustration of the way in which Paul's own use of εἴ γε would be understood by his contemporaries, and so provide at least an indirect indication of its meaning in the genuine letters. In Eph. iv 20-21 we have: ὑμεῖς δὲ οὐχ οὕτως ἐμάθετε τὸν Χριστόν· εἴ γε αὐτὸν ἠκούσατε καὶ ἐν αὐτῷ ἐδιδάχθητε καθώς ἐστιν ἀλήθεια ἐν τῷ Ἰησοῦ. This can hardly be intended to express a serious doubt as to the instruction the readers have received in the Christian faith. In Eph. i 13 they have been described as ἀκούσαντες τὸν λόγον τῆς ἀληθείας, which would seem to be the equivalent of αὐτὸν ἠκούσατε . . . καθώς ἐστιν ἀλήθεια ἐν τῷ Ἰησοῦ. The sense of εἴ γε is probably, "At any rate if you have heard . . . as I know you have." The other instance, Eph. iii 2, can be understood in the same way, although the construction here is obscure, owing to the circumstance that there is no very obvious apodosis. The clause εἴ γε ἠκούσατε τὴν οἰκονομίαν τῆς χάριτος τοῦ θεοῦ τῆς δοθείσης μοι εἰς ὑμᾶς is shortly followed by καθὼς προέγραψα ἐν ὀλίγῳ, which indicates that the contents of the εἴ γε clause are at least to some extent true.

Finally, there is one very interesting example in Romans: ἡ δὲ ἐλπὶς οὐ καταισχύνει, ὅτι ἡ ἀγάπη τοῦ θεοῦ ἐκκέχυται ἐν ταῖς καρδίαις ἡμῶν διὰ πνεύματος ἁγίου τοῦ δοθέντος ἡμῖν· εἴ γε Χριστὸς ὄντων ἡμῶν ἀσθενῶν ἔτι κατὰ καιρὸν ὑπὲρ ἀσεβῶν ἀπέθανεν (Rom. v 5-6). Here εἴ γε is the reading of B; other readings occur as follows:

ἔτι γάρ (+ ἔτι post ἀσθενῶν)	אACD* Sy.hl. Mcion
ἔτι (here only)	Dcω Chr. al.
εἰς τί γάρ	Db G lat Iren.lat. Ambst.
εἰ γάρ	201 Isid.-Pelus. Aug.
εἰ γὰρ . . . ἔτι	Sy.pal.
εἰ . . . ἔτι	Cop.sah.
εἰ γὰρ ἔτι	Cop.boh.
εἰ δέ	Sy.pesh.

The reading ἔτι γάρ has little to recommend it, for there seems to be no very good reason why it should have been altered. The only difficulty it presents is that of the double occurrence of ἔτι, and this would be readily eliminated simply by omitting the word later in the verse. And while the reading εἰ γάρ might possibly be derived from ἔτι γάρ as the result of a transcriptional error, this is unlikely to be the explanation of εἴ γε in B, partly because of the general reliability of B itself and partly because γε is so much less frequent than γάρ that it is hardly likely to have been written in mistake for it. If we eliminate ἔτι γάρ from consideration, we can also dismiss the two readings which appear to be derived from it; the reading ἔτι is presumably caused by the accidental omission of γάρ, and εἰς τί γάρ is likewise a transcriptional error of some kind. The basic choice, therefore, is between εἴ γε and εἰ γάρ. The readings εἰ . . . ἔτι and εἰ δέ are clearly derived from one or the other of these; in the first instance either γε or γάρ has been omitted, perhaps accidentally or perhaps in an attempt to emend the text; in the second it would seem that δέ has been substituted for γε, either by mistake or because γε was felt to give a wrong sense. Both εἴ γε and εἰ γάρ are difficult, and each could well have given rise to the other readings. If εἰ γάρ is original it lacks an apodosis. This might have been remedied in B by emending connective γάρ to non-connective γε, and so attaching the clause syntactically to the preceding sentence, and in ℵ and other witnesses by substituting ἔτι for εἰ and so eliminating the awkward protasis. On the other hand, an original εἴ γε would cause difficulties because the γε might be felt to suggest a doubt as to the truth of the following statement that Christ died on behalf of the ungodly. The first stage in the development of the variant would then be the somewhat thought-less emendation of γε to γάρ. This, in turn, would bring about the substitution of ἔτι for εἰ, in order to get rid of the syntactical difficulty of εἰ γάρ. In view of the problems presented by both readings, it is impossible to select either one as original on the grounds of its greater difficulty. But the attestation of B, even though unsupported, is good evidence in favor of εἴ γε, more especially since in II Cor. v 3 ms. B prefers the more confident εἴπερ to the less assured εἴ γε, which suggests that its editors would be unlikely of their own accord to use εἴ γε as the preface to a statement the truth of which is fundamental to Pauline theology. If, however, we accept the reading εἴ γε, the conclusion follows that Paul could use the combination to introduce a fact of which he was absolutely certain; in this particular instance we might paraphrase: "At any rate if Christ died on behalf of the ungodly—as we are convinced he did."

If, therefore, Pauline usage elsewhere is any guide to the meaning of εἴ γε in II Cor. v 3, there is a substantial possibility that it should be regarded as expressing assurance rather than doubt. In Rom. v 6 εἴ γε cannot in any circumstances indicate doubt, and in the three examples in Colossians and Ephesians the context suggests that the tone of the particles is confident. The only example which plainly expresses doubt is Gal. iii 4.

(c) There are two instances of εἴ γε in secular literature which show that it was possible to use the combination to introduce a statement of which the validity was not in question: οὐκ οὖν ὅπερ κύνα ποιεῖ καλόν, τοῦτο ἵππον αἰσχρόν, ὅπερ δ' ἵππον καλόν, τοῦτο κύνα αἰσχρόν, εἴ γε διάφοροι αἱ φύσεις εἰσὶν αὐτῶν; (Epict. Dss. III 1, 4). That the dog and the horse do in fact have differing natures has already been stated: ἐπειδὴ πρὸς ἄλλο μὲν ὁρῶμεν κύνα πεφυκότα, πρὸς ἄλλο δ' ἵππον (ibid. 1, 3). The other example is οἱ δέ, ἂν ἔχωσι, μὴ ἀναδυέσθωσαν, εἴ γε ἁρμόττει τὸν μὲν μὴ τῷ δύνασθαι καταχρῆσθαι πρὸς τὸ αὐθαδέστερον ἐφ' ὕβρει τῶν δανεισαμένων, τοὺς δὲ πρὸς ὑπόμνησιν τῆς τῶν ἀλλοτρίων ἀποδόσεως ἄξια παρέχειν ἐνέχυρα (Philo, de Virt. xvi).

This second set of arguments carries more weight than those which suggest that εἴ γε expresses doubt. Specifically Pauline usage, which possesses also some support in Hellenistic literature and the κοινή, is a more certain guide to the exegesis of II Cor. v 3 than either the function of γε in general or the interpretation of the verse by later scribes. It is true that the one Pauline instance of εἴ γε which does indicate doubt appears to be a more exact parallel to II Cor. v 3 than the other four which express confidence, since in both II Cor. v 3 and Gal. iii 4 εἴ γε is followed by καί. But in neither case is καί integrally attached to the preceding particles; in Gal. iii 4 it adheres to the following εἰκῆ, and in II Cor. v 3 it probably emphasizes ἐνδυσάμενοι. This use of καί to emphasize a word repeated from the previous sentence is a common Pauline idiom and is by no means restricted to clauses introduced by εἴ γε (see I Cor. iv 7; vii 11; Phil. iii 12; iv 10). There is therefore no reason to suppose that we have in these two verses some distinctive use of εἴ γε which must be interpreted in precisely the same way in both. The exactness of the parallel is illusory, and we are free to accept for II Cor. v 3 the sense of εἴ γε which is most frequent in the

Pauline writings, if this should give the more satisfactory sense to the passage as a whole.

Thus, it appears that Hettlinger's exegesis of εἴ γε can, after all, be justified on linguistic grounds, and that it is allowable to paraphrase the clause: "At any rate if we shall not be found to be disembodied—as I am sure we shall not."

A further argument against regarding εἴ γε as expressing doubt is simply that, if it does so, the sentence, strictly translated, makes very little sense: "At any rate if, having put on our heavenly body, we shall not be found naked—although I am afraid we may." Robinson avoids this difficulty by translating ἐνδυσάμενοι as though it were a perfect participle: "If, indeed, it *is* as clothed (*i.e.*, still alive), and not naked, that we shall be found (*sc.*, at the *Parousia*)." [1] Grammatically this is obviously incorrect. [2] There might conceivably be some justification for it if the perfect participle of the verb had in actual fact passed out of current use, but the New Testament itself shows that this was not so (see Mt. xxii 11; Mk. i 6; Rev. i 13; xv 6; xix 14).

The interpretation of εἴ γε as expressing assurance would seem to remove from verse 3, at any rate, the suggestion that Paul fears he may have to endure a period of disembodiment, and indeed to turn the verse into a positive assertion that the Christian believer will not be disembodied. It may be of interest to take this positive assertion as a basis for the exegesis of the whole section and to see whether the other ideas in the chapter can be reconciled with it.

Its primary and obvious advantage would appear at first sight to be that it harmonizes with the attitude to death which is found in verse 8. It must be pointed out, however, that if Robinson's interpretation of ἐπενδύσασθαι in verse 2 is correct, there is still a conflict between the ideas of the first half of the section and those of the second. He would take ἐπενδύσασθαι to mean "being clothed with the resurrection body at the *Parousia* while still alive." [3] Verse 3 would then imply merely that the fulfilment of the desire for this experience would preclude the possibility of existence in a disembodied state: "We long to be clothed with the resurrection body while still alive, since, having undergone this process, we

---

[1] *Op. cit.*, p. 77.
[2] Cf. Hettlinger's article, p. 178.
[3] *Op. cit.*, p. 77.

shall not find ourselves disembodied." The further implication would still be that there was a prospect of disembodiment for believers dying before the *Parousia*. And if εἴ γε is taken as expressing the assurance that this will not happen to Paul and his readers there is a conflict both with verse 1 and with verses 8-10, which suggest the contrary. Further, although verse 3 would no longer actively express the fear of disembodiment, it would nevertheless remain implicitly in the background. The only solution of the problem would be to reject this particular interpretation of ἐπενδύσασθαι. There is some justification for doing so, in that Robinson's exegesis of the first two verses is to some extent self-contradictory. He refers the οἰκοδομή ἐκ θεοῦ of verse 1 to the Body of Christ, and stresses the present tense ἔχομεν, implying that even though a Christian should die before the *Parousia* he will possess this heavenly dwelling at death. But in verse 2 the οἰκητή-ριον ἐξ οὐρανοῦ has become the resurrection body for the possession of which believers, alive or dead, must wait until the *Parousia*. [1] It is surely highly improbable that two so completely synonymous terms should be used in two different senses in adjacent verses. But if the οἰκητήριον of verse 2 is the same as the οἰκοδομή of verse 1, there is no reason to refer ἐπενδύσασθαι to the moment of the *Parousia*. It will refer to the moment of physical death, as does the ἔχομεν of verse 1, and the first two verses, as Hettlinger maintains, [2] will speak of a further incorporation into the Body of Christ which happens to the Christian at death. Verse 3, if εἴ γε expresses assurance, will confirm this, and justify the believer's longing for this event, by asserting that for the Christian the prospect of disembodiment at death is excluded. The first three verses are thus harmonized with verses 8-10.

There remains the minor difficulty, which has been mentioned already, [3] that if Hettlinger's interpretation of verses 1-3 is adopted the ἐνδυσάμενοι of verse 3 appears to be tautologous. It may not be out of place at this point to suggest an alternative meaning for it. Hettlinger refers it to the moment of death. But could it not equally well refer to the moment of baptism? Two of the Pauline occurrences of the verb are specifically baptismal; ὅσοι γὰρ εἰς Χριστὸν ἐβαπ-

---

[1] *Ibid.*, pp. 76-77.
[2] See his article, p. 189.
[3] See above, p. 86.

τίσθητε Χριστὸν ἐνεδύσασθε (Gal. iii 27), and ἀπεκδυσάμενοι τὸν παλαιὸν ἄνθρωπον . . . καὶ ἐνδυσάμενοι τὸν νέον . . . . (Col. iii 9-10); cf. ἐν τῇ ἀπεκδύσει τοῦ σώματος τῆς σαρκός, ἐν τῇ περιτομῇ τοῦ Χριστοῦ, συνταφέντες αὐτῷ ἐν τῷ βαπτίσματι . . . (Col. ii 11). All the other instances—apart from I Cor. xv 53-54, where ἐνδύσασθαι is used of the final clothing with the resurrection body at the *Parousia*—may very well be understood to refer to the Christian's gradual appropriation of the effects of his baptism (Rom. xiii 12, 14; Eph. iv 24; vi 11, 14; Col. iii 12; I Thess. v 8). The context in II Cor. v is suitable to a baptismal reference if the οἰκοδομὴ ἐκ θεοῦ refers to the Body of Christ; and there is also an implicit mention of baptism in verse 5, ὁ δοὺς ἡμῖν τὸν ἀρραβῶνα τοῦ πνεύματος. If this interpretation of ἐνδυσάμενοι is plausible, we might paraphrase verses 2-3 as follows: "We long to be freed from this present physical body and to put on our heavenly dwelling. (This longing for physical death is comprehensible) since having already put on the Body of Christ in baptism, we are convinced that we shall not be disembodied at death." By referring ἐνδυσάμενοι and the impossibility of being γυμνοί to two different moments, the tautology is removed.

Two apparent objections to this exegesis are provided by verse 4, and must be considered before it can be accepted. First, if the καὶ γάρ of verse 4 refers to the immediately preceding clause, verse 3 must be supposed to contain something to which the mention of depression in the following verse could be related, and the only possibility, from this point of view, would be the expression of a real fear of disembodiment. This is not, however, a very serious objection. There is no difficulty in referring καὶ γάρ to the longing for the heavenly dwelling which is expressed in verse 2, and in treating verse 3 as parenthetical in respect of the following connective. There are two other occasions in the Corinthian Epistles when γάρ does not refer to the immediately preceding sentence but to some statement further back in the argument; in II Cor. viii 9 γάρ refers to ἵνα καὶ ἐν ταύτῃ τῇ χάριτι περισσεύητε in verse 7, and in I Cor. xii 14 the phrase καὶ γὰρ τὸ σῶμα οὐκ ἔστιν ἓν μέλος ἀλλὰ πολλά refers to verse 12 (καθάπερ γὰρ τὸ σῶμα ἕν ἐστιν καὶ μέλη πολλὰ ἔχει . . . οὕτως καὶ ὁ Χριστός). The second objection is more substantial. If ἐφ' ᾧ means "because," as in Rom. v 12, then the phrase βαρούμενοι ἐφ' ᾧ οὐ θέλομεν ἐκδύσασθαι must be translated, "depressed because we do not want to be unclothed." This, in turn, implies the fear of nakedness and suggests that it may, after all, be present in verse 3 as well. In any case, the conflict with verse 8 remains unresolved. This difficulty is not to be avoided by displacing the negative. But is it absolutely certain that ἐφ' ᾧ means "because"? Is it not possible to understand it in its classical sense, "on condition that"? [1] This possibility seems to be disregarded by the grammarians and commentators, but if "on condition that" improves the sense, it is difficult to see why it should not be considered. The papyri provide several examples of ἐφ' ᾧ with this function, e.g. ἐφ' ὧι ... ποιήσεται τὴν τῆς μητρὸς κηδίαν καὶ περιστολὴν ὡς καθήκει (P. Tebt. II 381, 16). [2] It is clear, therefore, that the classical idiom survived into the κοινή. It is true that in II Cor. v 4 ἐφ' ᾧ is followed by the present indicative, whereas classical usage, retained in the papyri, requires the future tense. The meaning of the phrase, however, is future in some sense, as a verb of wishing by its nature implies the fixing of attention upon the point in the future when the wish is to be fulfilled, so that the present tense of θέλω may not be a real obstacle to the translation of ἐφ' ᾧ as "on condition that." It is worth pointing out that ἐφ' ᾧ is not in every instance causal elsewhere in the Pauline Epistles; in Phil. iv 10 the translation "because" makes very little sense, and some such phrase as "in which respect," "with regard to which," [3] would be preferable. And if Paul can use ἐφ' ᾧ in at least two different senses, [4] it is not inconceivable that he should use it in a third, if the third sense is possible linguistically. At any rate, the translation "on condition that" in II Cor. v 4 makes good sense and removes the difficulty. The verse would then mean: "For indeed, we who exist in the physical body groan with weariness. (But, for the Christian, this is a legitimate attitude to our physical existence only) on condition that we do not want to be divested of somatic existence altogether, but rather to be further incorporated in the Body of Christ." The ἐφ' ᾧ clause thus becomes a caution against the kind of Gnosticism which regarded the disembodied state as the ideal, and so would misunderstand the preceding reference to physical weariness.

---

[1] See Kühner-Gerth, *Ausführliche Grammatik der griechischen Sprache*, Hannover and Leipzig, 1904, II, ii, p. 505.

[2] Cf. P. Oxy. I 275 and P. Tebt. I 108, 4. (See Moulton and Milligan, *Vocab.*, *in loc.*, for the second of these examples and the one quoted in the text, and Robertson, *Grammar*, p. 963, for the first example).

[3] See C. F. D. Moule, *Idiom Book*, p. 132.

[4] The undoubtedly causal use occurs in Rom. v 12.

If this interpretation is plausible, the supposed references to the fear of disembodiment at death disappear. The εἴ γε clause in verse 3 becomes a positive assertion that for the Christian this fear is excluded, and the ἐφ' ᾧ clause in verse 4 becomes a warning against the desire to be disembodied. There is therefore no discrepancy between verses 3-4 and verse 8.

CONCLUSION

It remains to summarize briefly the conclusions arrived at in the preceding study and in some cases to suggest the possibility of further investigation.

The various tendencies exhibited by the κοινή with respect to the use of particles are conveniently exemplified in the New Testament writings. There is a marked decline in the use of the classical combinations of particles, but this is offset to some extent by other, more positive, tendencies which may be viewed as a sign of linguistic growth; a few new combinations make their appearance, some particles develop fresh functions, and new connecting particles are formed from other parts of speech. There is also a tendency for particles to change their position; some which in classical Greek take the second place in the sentence are found in the κοινή in the initial position, and γε in combination with other particles tends to cohere with them with no intervening word. It would be of interest to discover whether there is any earlier extant literature in which one might observe the beginnings of these linguistic processes, and there are some indications that the use of particles by Aristotle might be worth investigation in this connection. Mayser remarks that by comparison with Plato his style is deficient in collocations of particles, and it has been observed here that his writings provide examples of exceptive ἀλλά and of a use of ἀλλ' ἤ which is almost indistinguishable from that of adversative ἀλλά, both of which idioms are found in the κοινή. Moreover, the Pauline Epistles provide two examples of the Aristotelian use of τε γάρ, without a following τε or καί, in the sense of καὶ γάρ, [1] namely ἀλλὰ τὴν ἁμαρτίαν οὐκ ἔγνων εἰ μὴ διὰ νόμου· τήν τε γὰρ ἐπιθυμίαν οὐκ ἤδειν εἰ μὴ ὁ νόμος ἔλεγεν· οὐκ ἐπιθυμήσεις (Rom. vii 7), and εἴ τις πέποιθεν ἑαυτῷ Χριστοῦ εἶναι, τοῦτο λογιζέσθω πάλιν ἐφ᾽ ἑαυτοῦ ὅτι καθὼς αὐτὸς Χριστοῦ, οὕτως καὶ ἡμεῖς. ἐάν τε γὰρ περισσότερόν τι καυχήσωμαι περὶ τῆς ἐξουσίας ἡμῶν . . . οὐκ αἰσχυνθήσομαι (II Cor. x 7-8). Denniston gives a number of instances in Aristotle, one of which may be quoted in full for the sake of illustration: ἀνάγκη δὲ πολιτευομένους οὕτω πολιτεύεσθαι καλῶς (αἵ τε γὰρ ἀρχαὶ αἰεὶ διὰ τῶν βελτίστων ἔσονται τοῦ δήμου βουλομένου καὶ τοῖς ἐπιεικέσιν οὐ φθονοῦν-

---

[1] See Denn., p. 536.

τος), καὶ τοῖς ἐπιεικέσι καὶ γνωρίμοις ἀρκοῦσαν εἶναι ταύτην τὴν τάξιν
(*Pol.* 1318 b 33). This use of τε γάρ is not found elsewhere in the New
Testament and I have not been able to discover any external
examples, but it is just possible that it may have been current in
the κοινή, and that its appearance in Aristotle marks the starting-
point of the idiom.

From the exegetical point of view it has become clear that
attempts to attach some special, non-linguistic, significance to
the use of δέ and γάρ in Mark are unconvincing. The examination
of the particles in a selection of individual verses produces the
following rather miscellaneous results. Matthew shows a tendency
to diminish the impression of conflict apparent in the Marcan
account of Christ's prayer before his arrest (Mt. xxvi 39). On the
other hand, his supposed alteration of Jesus' reply to the High
Priest may be in fact an exact reproduction of Mark's plain affirmative (Mt. xxvi 64). The study of Paul's somewhat ambiguous
instruction to Christian slaves (I Cor. vii 21) has suggested that he
intended them to take advantage of an offer of freedom, and a
consideration of the use of εἴ γε in II Cor. v 3 leads to the conclusion
that the apparent contradiction in the first ten verses of this chapter
is capable of resolution, and that it is not necessary to suppose
that Paul feared an interval of disembodiment for Christians
dying before the *Parousia*. This aspect of the use of particles hardly
seems susceptible of further investigation, since the relative paucity
of particles exhibited by the New Testament as a whole reduces
the number of exegetical problems which depend upon their interpretation.

APPENDIX

A. *Combinations of Particles*

(i) PLATO: *Apology*

ἀλλ' ἄρα, ἀλλὰ γάρ, ἀλλὰ . . . γε, ἀλλὰ δή, ἀλλ' οὖν . . . γε, ἄρ' οὖν, γὰρ δή, γὰρ δήπου . . . γε, γὰρ οὖν, γάρ τοι, γε δή, γοῦν, δὲ ἄρα, δέ γε, δὲ δή, δὲ καί, δ' οὖν, δὴ οὖν, δήπου, εἴτε δή, εἴτ' οὖν, ἐπειδήπερ γε, εἴπερ γε, ἦ μήν, καὶ γάρ, καὶ . . . γε, καὶ . . . δή, καὶ δὴ καί, καὶ μέντοι καί, καίπερ, καίτοι, καίτοι . . . γε, μὲν δή, μὲν οὖν, μέντοι, μέντοι . . . γε, οὐδὲ γάρ, οὐδὲ γάρ . . . δήπου, οὐδέ γε, τε μέντοι.

NEW TESTAMENT

ἀλλὰ καί, ἀλλ' οὐδέ, ἄρα γε, ἄρά γε, γὰρ δήπου, γάρ που, δὲ καί, ἐπειδήπερ, καθάπερ καί, καὶ γάρ, καὶ . . . γε, καὶ . . . δέ, καίπερ, καίτοιγε, μὲν οὖν, μέντοι, οὐδὲ γάρ, τε γάρ, τοιγαροῦν.

XENOPHON: *Institutio Cyri* I

ἀλλὰ . . . γάρ, ἀλλὰ . . . γε, ἀλλὰ καί, ἀλλὰ μέντοι, ἀλλὰ μήν, ἀλλ' οὐδέ, ἀλλά τοι, ἄρά γε, γὰρ δή, γὰρ δήπου, γὰρ οὖν, γε δή, γε μήν, γοῦν, δ' ἄρα, δέ γε, δὲ δή, δ' οὖν, δήπου, ἦ καί, καὶ γάρ τοι, καὶ . . . γε, καὶ μὲν δή, καίτοι, καὶ τοίνυν, μέν γε, μὲν δή, μὲν δήπου, μὲν οὖν, μέντοι, μέντοι γε, οὐδὲ γάρ, οὐδέ γε.

ACTS OF THE APOSTLES

ἀλλὰ καί, ἀλλ' οὐδέ, ἄρα γε, ἄρά γε, δὲ καί, καὶ γάρ, μὲν οὖν, οὐδὲ γάρ.

PHILOSTRATUS: *Vita Apollonii* I

ἀλλὰ . . . γε, ἀλλὰ . . . δή, ἀλλὰ καί, γὰρ δή, γάρ που, γε μήν, γοῦν, δὲ ἄρα, δέ γε, δὲ δή, δὲ καί, δ' οὖν, δήπου, ἦ γάρ, καὶ γάρ, καὶ . . . γε, καὶ . . . δέ, καὶ δή, καὶ δῆτα, καὶ μήν, καὶ μὴν καί, καί που, καίτοι, μὲν δή, μὲν οὖν, μέντοι, οὐδὲ γάρ, οὐ μήν . . . γε.

(ii) PAPYRI

ἀλλὰ καί, ἀλλ' οὐδέ, γάρ που, δ' ἄρα, δέ γε, δὲ καί, δ' οὖν, δήπου, εἴπερ γε δή, εἴτε δή, εἴτε καί, ἦ μήν, καθάπερ καί, καὶ γάρ, καὶ . . . δέ, καὶ δή, καίπερ, καίτοι, καίτοι γε, μὲν οὖν, μέντοι, μέντοι γε, οὐδὲ γάρ, οὐδὲ . . . γε, οὐδὲ μήν, οὐ μὴν ἀλλά, οὐ μὴν ἀλλά . . . γε, οὔτε δή, τε δή.

EPICTETUS: *Discourses* I-IV

ἀλλά . . . γε, ἀλλά καί, ἀλλά μήν, ἀλλ᾽ οὐδέ, ἀλλ᾽ οὖν, ἄρά γε,
ἄρ᾽ οὖν, γὰρ δή . . . γε, γοῦν, δ᾽ ἄρα, δέ γε, δὲ δή, δὲ καί, δ᾽ οὖν,
δήπου, καθάπερ καί, καὶ γάρ, καὶ . . . δέ, καὶ μήν, καὶ μήν γε,
καίτοι, καίτοι . . . γε, καὶ τοίνυν, μέν γε, μὲν οὖν, μέντοι, οὐδὲ γάρ,
τοιγαροῦν, τοιγάρτοι.

HERMETICA

ἀλλὰ δή, ἀλλὰ καί, ἀλλὰ μήν, ἀλλ᾽ οὐδέ, ἀλλ᾽ οὐδὲ μήν, γὰρ
δήπου, γάρ που, γάρ τοι, γοῦν, δ᾽ ἄρα, δὲ καί, δὴ οὖν, διόπερ καί,
ἐπειδήπερ, ἦ γάρ, καθάπερ καί, καὶ γάρ, καὶ . . . δέ, καὶ δὴ καί,
καίπερ, καίτοι, μέν γε, μὲν δή, μὲν οὖν, μέντοι, οὐδὲ γάρ, οὐδὲ οὖν,
τοιγαροῦν, τοιγάρτοι.

(iii) MENANDER: *Dyskolos*

ἀλλὰ γάρ, ἀλλὰ καί, ἀλλὰ μήν, ἄρά γε, γὰρ δῆτα, γοῦν, δέ γε, δὲ
δή, δὲ καί, καὶ γάρ, καὶ . . . γε, καὶ δή, καὶ μήν, μὲν οὖν, μέντοι,
οὐδὲ γάρ, οὐ μὴν ἀλλά . . . γε, τοιγαροῦν.

ARISTOPHANES: *Clouds*, 1-956

ἀλλά . . . γε, ἀλλ᾽ οὐδέ, ἀλλ᾽ οὐδ᾽ . . . μέντοι . . . γε, ἄρά γε,
ἀτάρ . . . γε, γὰρ δή, γὰρ δή . . . γε, γάρ . . . δῆτα, γάρ τοι, γε μήν,
γέ τοι, γέ τοι δή, γοῦν, δ᾽ ἄρα, δέ γε, δὲ καί, δ᾽ οὖν, δή γε, δήπου,
δῆτ᾽ οὖν, εἴπερ . . . γε, εἴτε ἄρα, ἦ μήν, καὶ . . . γε, καὶ δή, καὶ
μήν . . . γε, καίπερ, καίτοι, καίτοι . . . γε, μὲν . . . γε, μὲν οὖν,
μέντοι, οὐδὲ γάρ, οὐδέ γε, οὐ δῆτα . . . γε, οὐ μήν . . . γε, οὖν δῆτα,
τε δή.

(iv) *Classical Combinations*

PAULINE EPISTLES

ἀλλὰ καί, ἀλλ᾽ οὐδέ, δὲ καί, καθάπερ καί, καὶ γάρ, καὶ . . . γε,
καὶ . . . δέ, καίπερ, μὲν οὖν, οὐδὲ γάρ, τε γάρ, τοιγαροῦν.

EPICTETUS: *Discourses* I

ἀλλὰ καί, ἀλλὰ μήν, ἀλλ᾽ οὐδέ, ἀλλ᾽ οὖν, ἄρα γε, ἄρ᾽ οὖν, γοῦν,
δ᾽ ἄρα, δὲ καί, δ᾽ οὖν, καθάπερ καί, καὶ γάρ, καὶ μήν, καὶ μήν . . .
γε, καίτοι, καίτοι . . . γε, καὶ . . . τοίνυν, μὲν οὖν, οὐ γὰρ δή γε,
οὐδὲ γάρ.

POLYBIUS I

γε μήν, δὲ καί, δ᾽ οὖν, καθάπερ καί, καὶ γάρ, καὶ μήν, μὲν οὖν,
μέντοι γε, οὐδὲ μήν, οὐ μὴν ἀλλά, οὐ μήν . . . γε, τε δή, τοιγαροῦν.

EPISTLE TO THE HEBREWS

ἀλλὰ καί, γὰρ δήπου, γάρ που, καθάπερ καί, καὶ γάρ, καίπερ, καίτοι, μὲν οὖν, τοιγαροῦν.

B. καί γε *in Acts*

There are three examples of this idiom in Acts, but in each instance there is a textual variant, and the acceptance of the reading καί γε needs some justification.

(a) καί γε ἐπὶ τοὺς δούλους μου καὶ ἐπὶ τὰς δούλας μου ἐν ταῖς ἡμέραις ἐκείναις ἐκχεῶ ἀπὸ τοῦ πνεύματός μου (Acts ii 18).

In this verse J. H. Ropes prints καὶ ἐγ[ὼ] as the reading of D. [1] As a transcription of the existing text of D there appears to be little warrant for this: the letters ΓΕ following ΚΑΙ are fairly clear. But there are two considerations which may suggest that D originally had the reading chosen by Ropes. First, the spacing shows that a different word may have been written in the place of γε and later corrected, since there is a small gap after ΚΑΙ and another before ΕΠΙ. Secondly, the text of *d* has "et ego," and there is some evidence that this is derived from D and not from the Greek original of *d* itself; the text of *d* is most akin to the text of *gig*, [2] and *gig* supports καί γε with the reading "et quidem." It is thus probable that the scribe of D first wrote καὶ ἐγώ, and therefore it is necessary to consider whether he was preserving the original reading of Acts ii 18 in doing this or whether he was simply making a mistake or indulging in alteration or gratuitous and misplaced correction.

The first alternative is unlikely for two reasons. It is difficult to understand why the author of Acts should have introduced a super-fluous ἐγώ into his quotation from Joel iii 2. The emphasis is not so much upon the fact that it is God who gives the Spirit as upon the actual event of the Spirit's outpouring and the accompanying phenomena, and in any case an emphasis upon the giver of the Spirit would come more naturally at the beginning of the quotation rather than halfway through. On the other hand, it is comparatively easy to account for the addition of γε to the text of the Septuagint; καί γε is frequent in the Septuagint in general and the author of Luke-Acts is obviously familiar with Septuagintal style and so may

---

[1] *The Beginnings of Christianity*, Pt. I, Vol. III, *The Text of Acts*.
[2] *Ibid.*, p. cxi.

have automatically written καί γε where the source for his quotation has simply καί.[1] Secondly, the widespread attestation of καί γε is hard to account for except on the supposition that it is the original reading. If the variant had originated in a transcriptional error one would hardly expect the incorrect reading to be so universally current. On the other hand, if it is a question of conscious alteration it is difficult to see why this should result in so unanimous an adoption of καί γε. The omission of ἐγώ might very well take place simultaneously in several branches of the textual tradition in order to bring about conformity with the text of the Septuagint, but this does not explain the introduction of γε. Even if some witnesses were to add γε, for the sake, perhaps, of avoiding hiatus, one would expect others to retain the simple καί. It seems preferable, therefore, to accept καί γε as the original reading, and to suppose that the original reading in D was a transcriptional error which was later corrected.

(b) In Acts xiv 16-17 the text of D has: ὃς ἐν ταῖς παρῳχημέναις γενεαῖς εἴασε πάντα τὰ ἔθνη πορεύεσθαι ταῖς ὁδοῖς αὐτῶν· καί γε οὐκ ἀμάρτυρον ἀφῆκεν ἑαυτὸν ἀγαθοποιῶν. The reading καί γε is supported also by P⁴⁵ E d gig. On the other hand, BAC ℵᶜ 81 read καίτοι, and ℵ*HLP have καίτοιγε.

Working on the principle of giving preference to the more difficult reading one would obviously come to the conclusion that καί γε is original. The relation between the two sentences quoted is adversative, and immediately suggests καίτοι as a suitable connective. The suitability of καί γε, on the other hand, is less apparent; in the few secular examples which have been quoted the καί (where it acts as a connective) has a purely progressive function. If this is so, however, it is necessary to ask whether the original author is likely to have written καί γε in the first place, or whether the more difficult reading is too difficult to be plausible at all. Here it is relevant to point out that the Septuagint occasionally uses καί γε in an adversative sense. There are the following examples in the historical books: καὶ ἤγειρεν αὐτοῖς κύριος κριτὰς καὶ ἔσωσεν αὐτοὺς ἐκ χειρὸς τῶν προνομευόντων αὐτούς. καί γε τῶν κριτῶν αὐτῶν οὐκ ἐπήκουσαν. (Jg. ii 16-17); καὶ ὅτι ἀληθῶς ἀγχιστεὺς ἐγώ εἰμι, καί γε ἔστιν ἀγχιστεὺς ἐγγίων ὑπὲρ ἐμέ (Ruth iii 12); and καὶ ἐθυμώθη κύριος σφόδρα

---

[1] Some manuscripts of the Septuagint have καί γε here, but Rahlfs maintains that this reading is due to assimilation to Acts ii 18 (*Septuaginta*, ed. Alfred Rahlfs, Stuttgart, 1935, *in loc.*).

ἐν τῷ Ἰσραηλ καὶ ἀπέστησεν αὐτοὺς ἀπὸ τοῦ προσώπου αὐτοῦ, καὶ οὐχ ὑπελείφθη πλὴν φυλὴ Ἰουδα μονωτάτη. καί γε Ἰουδας οὐκ ἐφύλαξεν τὰς ἐντολὰς κυρίου τοῦ θεοῦ αὐτῶν (IV King. xvii 18-19; cf. also Jg. xix 18-19). It is possible that in Acts xiv 17 the author may have been influenced by the Septuagintal idiom, and thus may have used καί γε in an adversative sense. The unfamiliarity of this function of the collocation will have led to the substitution of the more obvious καίτοι in the majority of manuscripts.

(c) ζητεῖν τὸν θεόν, εἰ ἄρα γε ψηλαφήσειαν αὐτὸν καὶ εὕροιεν, καί γε οὐ μακρὰν ἀπὸ ἑνὸς ἑκάστου ἡμῶν ὑπάρχοντα (Acts xvii 27). The reading καί γε is supported by BD² (D* has καί τε, which would appear to be simply a transcriptional error) HLP* 81. As in the case of the previous variant καίτοι and καίτοιγε occur as an alternative: καίτοιγε אP²; καίτοι AE.

Again καί γε is the more difficult reading; there is no external supporting evidence for its use as a concessive particle introducing a participial clause. This does not, however, necessarily mean that the author of Acts could not have used it in this sense. If in Acts xiv 17 he used καί γε as the equivalent of καίτοι to introduce an independent sentence, he may also have used it as the equivalent of concessive καίτοι introducing a subordinate clause. It may be concluded, therefore, that καί γε is in all probability correct, especially as it is here attested by B.

INDEX OF PASSAGES

(1) NEW TESTAMENT

(5) PAPYRI